600 Heac

36 Ends per inch

36   Ends or headles needed
× 16. inches or width
─────
216
36
─────
576   headles

WEAVING AS AN ART FORM
A Personal Statement

Theo Moorman

Black and white photography by Nicholas Large
Color photography by John Walling

VNR **VAN NOSTRAND REINHOLD COMPANY**
New York Cincinnati Toronto London Melbourne

I wish to express my thanks to those people whose collaboration has made possible the production of this book. These are Margaret Harris, my secretary; Nicholas Large, whose excellent work on black and white photography of my hangings goes back over a number of years; John Walling, who has been responsible for the color photography for this book.

Among a group of close friends who have helped me in many ways, my thanks are especially due to my colleague, Eileen Chadwick, who has given me her invaluable advice, assistance, and encouragement throughout.

On the jacket: "Dark Form on Blue," wall hanging. 30 in. x 38 in. Linen and cotton.

Van Nostrand Reinhold Company Regional Offices:
New York   Cincinnati   Chicago   Millbrae   Dallas
Van Nostrand Reinhold Company International Offices:
London   Toronto   Melbourne

Published by Van Nostrand Reinhold Company
A Division of Litton Educational Publishing, Inc.
450 West 33rd Street, New York, N.Y. 10001
16 15 14 13 12 11 10 9 8 7 6 5 4 3 2 1

Library of Congress Cataloging in Publication Data

Moorman, Theo.
  Weaving as an art form.

  Includes index.
  1. Hand weaving. 2. Moorman, Theo. I. Title.
TT848.M66   746.3'92'4   74-18908
ISBN 0-442-26002-4

CONTENTS

". . . what constitutes the dignity of a craft is that it creates a fellowship, that it binds men together and fashions for them a common language. For there is but one veritable problem — the problem of human relations." — Antoine de Saint-Exupéry, *Wind, Sand and Stars*

INTRODUCTION

Born and bred in the shadow of a red brick university in the industrial north of England, the child of literary parents and with an academically brilliant elder brother, I developed, at the outset, a certain perverse and reactionary allergy to books. I remember clearly my first efforts to read. The story concerned some child with a watering can of whom the fate was then and is now a matter of supreme indifference to me. Could the doubtful benefits of literacy really be worth the effort involved? The sixty years that have elapsed since then have proved the error of this first impression, but I still have a lurking feeling that the world contains too many books. The decision to add one more to their number has not been made lightly. It springs from a desire to bring together and make some coherent sense out of my thoughts on the design and aesthetic expression embodied in a woven fabric, thoughts which have been circulating in my mind as I have pursued the practical work of weaving during the last decade. A day's weaving allows a good deal of time for thought, not only on the immediate matters related to the successful production of the work on the loom, but also on the wider and more fundamental problems involved in the design and production of woven objects.

The title and subtitle of this book, with the stress on the personal approach, are important. The convictions which I have reached on many points, and which I plan to enlarge on, have come to me empirically rather than analytically. Unfortunately for me, I seem, in my work as a weaver and designer, only able to gain ground through a mass of experiments, blunders, and muddles. With a few exceptions, only the weaving that I have produced in the last ten or fifteen years has, for me, any real merit or validity, and this shows the serious waste of time that can result from an inability to think a problem out, logically, from the roots upwards, rather than plunging in and only learning from the mistakes of impetuosity. For this reason it would clearly be presumptuous for me to write authoritatively on the basic and generally accepted principles of design and color. I only plan to share with fellow weavers and other craftsmen who may be interested in the subject ideas that have come to me personally, as a result of a long period of explorations and disappointments, experiences and discoveries.

Recently a little boy asked me, in the course of a conversation about this and that, how long I had been weaving. Without stopping to work out a precise answer, I said, "I suppose about fifty years." When I saw his open-eyed astonishment, I said, "Well, maybe not quite so long, perhaps about forty years." He replied, "Say forty — it sounds better." But does it? I feel rather grateful for the half-century of work and for the rich and rewarding experiences of that time. It is interesting to be in a position to look back and to be aware of the enormous changes in the accepted outlook on weaving and designing for weaving that have come about. Can the pace of change possibly continue to accelerate, or will there perforce be a period of deceleration and consolidation?

Nowadays weaving and the allied processes of manipulating thread and fiber are generally accepted as an art form, but this has only recently been so. The weaving class I attended as an art student in the twenties taught three subjects: yardage weaving for dress and furnishing fabrics, rug weaving, and tapestry weaving. Wall hangings had not been "invented," and everything was, of course, strictly flat and two-dimensional. Tapestry weaving was essentially a pictorial craft. Walter Taylor, the weaving instructor at the Central School of Arts and Crafts in London, where I studied, had started his career as one of William Morris's apprentices. No breach had at that time been made in the solid wall of tradition in European tapestry weaving that had stretched from the fourteenth to the beginning of the twentieth century. It was the accepted thing for tapestries to be woven in factories or weaving studios by craftsmen who were essentially interpreters rather than creators, but the designs for these works were produced by well-known artists. This set up a generally accepted pattern of, on the one hand, the craftsman, anonymous and retiring, and on the other, the artist, dominant, known, and named. He may be Raphael, whose famous cartoons for a series of Brussels tapestries are one of the great art treasures to be seen at the Victoria and Albert Museum in London or, in our own time, Graham Sutherland, whose painted design for the huge Christ in Majesty in Coventry Cathedral has been enlarged and meticulously reproduced in weaving, brushstroke by brushstroke, so that even the painted signature, blown up to ten times its natural size, spans at least a couple of yards of fabric. Of the weavers in the Aubusson factory where the work was made, we know little or nothing.

The comparatively recent emergence of the artist-designer-weaver, emphatically one person, seems to me to constitute a major breakthrough in the history of the craft. At last, in the splendid tapestries, hangings and woven sculptures now pouring out of many countries, we see works conceived from the outset in terms of spinning and weaving. We are aware of the deep and intimate appreciation of fibers, textures, and colors and the unique interplay between these elements and realize that such attributes can only occur when artist and weaver are one. No more interpretation by one man of another man's work, with all the irreparable loss of vitality and pungency that must occur in the translation, but one man's work growing from its own strong roots, the heat of the original concept carried direct from the heart of the work to its totality without the jolt and gap incurred in the process of handing over from painter to weaver.

The ensuing creativity in the form of three-dimensional weaving, with all the allied techniques such as wrapping, macramé, crochet, knitting, and many more, seems a logical and almost inevitable result of the emergence of the artist-craftsman, the one man in the dual role. When we reach the point where an artistic concept is united with an understanding of exactly how the work is to be produced and what materials are to go into its making, when, indeed, the artistic concept may grow out of this very knowledge, then a whole new creative field is bound to appear and original ideas will be born. This new advance in the textile world has come at a time when what used to be referred to as "the fine arts" — drawing, painting, and sculpture — have likewise broken out from the accepted traditions. In the textile arts the resultant outpouring of new works varies in quality from the fully convinced and controlled work of art as seen, perhaps, at its height in the products of some of the Polish weavers, to the muddled, tangled, undigested bid for novelty at all costs which, if we are honest, we must admit appears only too frequently in the innumerable exhibitions of textile arts of the present day. For let us be clear on one point: when we weavers join the ranks of artists we are plunging into the company of painters and sculptors of all time. However small, trivial, and insignificant our efforts, we are no longer in a backwater. We are out in the mainstream, whether we like it or not, and our aims, if they are to be in any sense valid, must be of the same essence as those of the great masters. We stand, minute and trembling, in the company of Michelangelo and Titian, of Turner and Henry Moore. Before you pronounce this claim exaggerated and far-fetched, stop to consider. If our work is devoid of all practical use, if it is not even a space divider or a door curtain, if it ceases to stop a draft or mask a window, its sole purpose is to enhance the beauty or significance of its setting. A wall hanging in a room fulfils the same essential function as a drawing or painting, even though it is far removed from either in appearance. It is intended to please and interest the eye and arouse thoughts and emotions in the mind. It has no other function, and if it fails in this, its value vanishes. The responsibility of the producer of a wall hanging or piece of textile sculpture is therefore very great, and, if we are striving to reach a high standard in our work, we must perforce face up bravely to this situation.

I want to make it quite clear that, in voicing this opinion, I am not in any way suggesting that a wall hanging must or even should have something that is commonly thought of as a pictorial quality. It can sometimes happen that sheer refined craftsmanship and sensitivity in the handling of beautiful natural materials will produce hangings which stand in their own right as works of art. Sometimes, again, the design concept may originate in a technical experiment, but the end product will far transcend mere technology. The constructive thought behind a macrogauze hanging by Peter Collingwood can produce a work capable of giving visual satisfaction in a profound and enduring way. The delight derived from such a work may be compared with our experience in the presence of a painting by Josef Albers or an abstract relief by Ben Nicholson. Alongside this cool and classical approach lies the warmer, romantic, evocative thought which supplies the background to the larger section of modern weaving. Textile artists nowadays seem, at times, almost intoxicated with the heady richness of fibers, yarns and dyestuffs. The voluptuous beauty of unwoven yarns, of unspun fleece, silk, flax, tow and jute, and all the other natural and synthetic materials at the disposal of the textile artist today can contribute to works of immense richness, depth, and lasting value when the weaver is a genuine artist, maintaining control of all this rich material, using it for his own ends; being, in fact, the god of the machine. It can also easily get out of control, producing a state of euphoria where an undigested tangle of richness can masquerade as a work of art.

It is clear that the new sense of freedom in the textile arts, as in wider issues, brings with it a new set of responsibilities. In this contemporary world, where selvedges ebb and flow, where warps can turn into wefts at the drop of a hat, and every form of found or natural object is meat to the hungry weaver — where many of us roam streets, woods, and shores with a roving and predatory eye, collecting detrita of all sorts to incorporate with our more traditional materials — the obligation to reflect, to control, to order these miscellaneous objects to obey us and take a correct place in our master plan becomes very great and very urgent. If we lose this control we are in grave danger of ending up with a strange and unorganized accumulation of trash rather than a work of art. Those weavers who adhere to traditional materials, who spin shining flax and soft natural fleeces, subsequently weaving them in the simplest possible way, can, within their own self-imposed limitations, hardly go wrong. Those, however, who venture beyond the safety of this exquisite walled garden into the rough and adventurous outside world need all the resolution they can muster if they are not to be battered on the rocks.

Here then is our dilemma — here is the problem with no answer or with many answers. What should be our own true goal? Should we aim at near perfection within the walled garden or should we go outside the door and face the tremendous pressures and buffetings waiting for us in the permissive and dangerous modern world? This is a world full of synthetic materials, of plastic in all forms, of ugliness, rebellion, and violence, of anti-art and anti-craft. It seems to me that this dilemma must be faced by serious modern craftsmen, and that the right answer can only be individual and personal to each of us. Our first duty is to be honest with ourselves.

It is interesting to see how many young people, faced with the great world problems of pollution, unbalance of natural forces, even stark threats of annihilation, are turning to producing, by the simplest means, the basic necessities of existence. In addition to the building of huts and shelters and the growing of food, some of these young people are spinning, weaving, and knitting their own garments and blankets from natural materials with a most honest urgency, quite divorced from any theoretical and idealistic plans to put the clock back. As Noah, hearing and seeing the waters rising, must have recognized the power put into his hands in the form of the simplest possible tools and materials, the hammers, nails, and planks of wood which were to save the living world, so perhaps spinners and weavers today treasure and revere their spinning wheels, looms, and fleeces when they hear the daily news that pours from radio and television.

The validity of these basic desires and interests cannot be overlooked in our absorption with the different aims of the experimenters, explorers, and discoverers. Many of these see yarns and fibers as legitimate art media, courageously taking on the whole gamut of new materials and ideas and allowing themselves to be swept into the turbulent rapids of present-day art, albeit hoping not to lose all control of their concepts, techniques, and materials in the process.

Between these two extremes, the serenity of the walled garden and the turbulence of the rapids, it is, of course, possible to compromise and find a middle position. The really important aim should be to embark on a project with the right motives. A woven object must relate to its environment, and in producing works specifically for an exhibition there is an element of artificiality which can be a danger. Although an exhibition can be a useful stimulus to creativity, it can also lead to the production of something dishonest. The thoughts of the best of us are capable of turning, shamefully, in the direction of going one better than our fellow exhibitors, and we can only too easily become involved in a concept which fails to spring from a true emotion.

It is apparent that today's conditions present us, above all, with a need for honesty, particularly for honesty with ourselves. We must train ourselves to select, from many possible lines of approach, the one that is right and fruitful for *us*, where our ideas can have a chance to grow strongly and naturally and where we can ourselves develop to our full stature as both artists and craftsmen. It never harms us to aim high. I believe that all of us have hidden subconscious creative springs and are capable of surprising ourselves, given the right stimulus. I have not only proved this in my own work and experience but have also seen it happening in the work of my students.

chapter 1

PERSONAL BACKGROUND

As I have already indicated, my personal approach is bound to play an important part in these writings. It seems appropriate, therefore, to give at this point some details of those periods and happenings in my life which influenced in a special way the development of my thoughts, aspirations, and productions. As I look back on a life devoted for the most part to weaving, these periods stand out as salient points.

Unfortunately, my official art education does not rank as one of them. Sent to the wrong school at the wrong age, I failed, sadly, to find my feet in any of three wasted years. This failure has caused me deep regret ever since. Had I but learned to draw, had I even learned what drawing was about, many of my subsequent struggles would have been alleviated. As it was, I drifted through this time, bored and frustrated. Only in weaving class did I find a measure of happiness. Here the practical teaching was probably the best available at that time but, as I look back, it seems as if any helpful instruction in design and aesthetics was minimal. At the end of this unfruitful period, I got, by a sort of miracle, a job which changed the course of my life, and through which I at last emerged into some daylight, was happy, and started to learn something.

Work at Heals

The well-known furniture store Heal and Son, Ltd., in Tottenham Court Road, London, was in those days a green and fertile oasis in an aesthetic desert. This enlightened firm had, from the start, set its face firmly in the direction of good design and fine craftsmanship. The spacious store was architecturally well planned and had an air about it that was signally lacking elsewhere in the 1920s. It would be difficult to name a period when furniture design reached its nadir, but I think that those years might have the strongest claim. Senseless over-ornamentation, baronial carved oak tortured and twisted and then coated in sticky stains and varnishes seemed the common taste of the day. Fabrics and carpets in stuffy colors and designs followed suit. Tottenham Court Road seemed full of shops selling such things, and there, suddenly and surprisingly, in the midst of them was Heals and to Heals I went, at the age of twenty-one, to weave rugs.

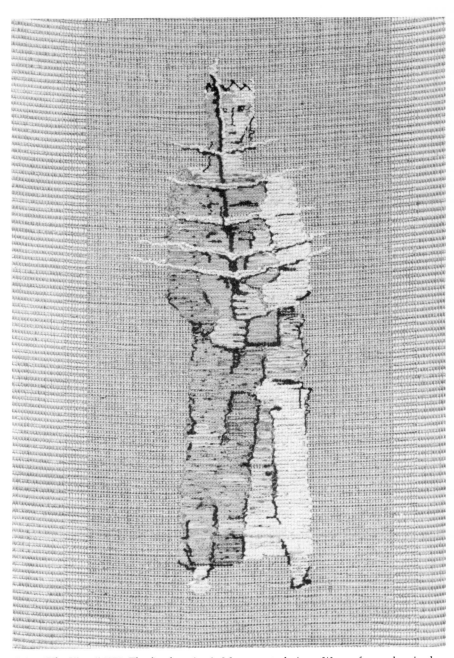

1-1. "The King," 1955. The first hanging in Moorman technique. Woven from a drawing by Austin Wright.

It was the policy of the firm to take on a number of graduate students from the leading London art schools to help in various ways both in the shop and in the craft studios attached to it. Thus it happened that, alongside the more conventional shop assistants, there was a group of boys and girls, artistic, talented, but abysmally inexperienced and unbusinesslike, working as near apprentices for minimal wages. I sometimes think we must have been a sore trial to the old hands and professionals, and certainly it was hard for us to learn business methods. I remember once getting a tremendous dressing-down for having worked overtime, but how was I to know that this was a crime? Interested in what I was doing and probably eager to see the final result of a piece of weaving, it seemed the most natural thing in the world to carry on in the peace and quiet of my own little studio, after my neighbors had gone home, until I reached that tense but irresistible moment of cutting a work off the loom and really seeing it for the first time (forty years later I still have the same reactions at this same moment). Practical work on the premises ranged from the highly professional production of beds and bedding for which the firm was justly famous, possibly the finest in the world at that time, to work on products from various studios tucked away around the premises, where furniture was painted, lampshades were made and decorated, cushions, bedspreads, and other articles were sewn and embroidered. Scribes also worked on the preparation of display cards, price tickets, and such things, the high quality of which contributed to the overall good appearance of the showrooms throughout the store. These people were my friends and colleagues, and among them I happily and proudly started work — at two pounds per week, which even in those days did not go very far. In the little canteen where we drank coffee and tea, conversations covered a whole range of subjects. (Among many interesting people taking part in these was Miss Smith, who, much to the excitement and glory of the shop, later emerged as Dodie Smith, famous author and playwright. I remember her witty comments as she crumbled biscuits in her tiny, nervous hands.)

Sir Ambrose Heal, Managing Director, alert, rosy of cheek, ginger of hair, blue and sparkling of eye, was a remote and high-up personage of whom I stood in considerable awe. Less remote were two remarkable women, both holding important positions in the business. These were rival queens. Prudence Maufe, wife of the famous architect who designed Guildford Cathedral, was handsome, ageless, solemn, and immensely dignified. She ruled over her own court in the exhibition gallery attached to the shop. I never remember her wearing anything but black dresses, cut with tight bodices and full, ankle-length skirts, beneath which square-toed black shoes, with silver buckles, were only just visible. Her strong and unusual personality and high ideals must have had a big influence on the policy and development of this remarkable business. My own queen, ruling over the embroidery studio to which my weaving room was attached, was Jeanetta Cochrane, distinguished theatrical dress designer. A London theater now bears her name. No one could have been in stronger contrast to Prudence Maufe. A big, sturdy woman, apple-cheeked and bright-eyed, with strong grizzled curly hair fanning out from a center parting, she resembled those lusty cherubs to be seen on eighteenth-century monuments. Her robust and irrepressible sense of humor and strong common sense swept over tense situations, splintering overcharged emotions and reducing them to laughter and to a cool and sane normality. In this respect I had more than one occasion to be grateful to her. If Prudence Maufe could have been described as having some affinity with the Pre-Raphaelites, Jeanetta Cochrane would have got on better with Smollett.

This rich variety of personalities, among whom I was to work for two valuable years with all the fun, loves, friendships, gossips, reprimands, and rows, provided a healthy climate in which young people had the right stimulus and opportunity to grow. The visual environment in which we worked was also exciting and educative. My academic family and school background had presented me with reproductions from the old masters which I dutifully admired, more because it seemed the right thing to do than from any deep conviction. Nothing could really have been more remote and unhelpful to a budding designer in the 1920s. At Heals we were surrounded by everyday things of good contemporary design. New ideas from Scandinavia were filtering into England at that time, and Heals, of course, was in the lead in the promotion and marketing of objects designed and made in those countries. The fact that this imaginative and enterprising policy overlaid a strong and shrewd business organization provided a basis of firm reality of which we were all aware, and I look back with gratitude to the all-round education I acquired in the time I spent with this firm. It made up a bit for my art school fiasco. As for the rugs I designed and made — well — it is a long time ago. Maybe at the time some of them were enjoyed by their owners. It is comforting to me to think how many years must have gone by since they ceased to exist.

Free-Lance Weaving — Phase One

After two years of this life I had had enough. My friends at Heals left for other jobs and I decided to branch out as a free-lance weaver. My single room in central London, which was, perhaps, twenty feet square, contained a bed and minimal equipment for living, a partitioned-off kitchen, a forty-inch horizontal loom, a large vertical rug loom, a warping mill, and other smaller weaving equipment as well as yarns, so work and life were both a bit cramped. Even when I moved to larger and more attractive premises my work was still restricted in many ways, but the thing that finally made me look for a change from Heals was my inability to get my hands on the yarns that I desired for my weaving. It is a sign today of the escalating interest in handweaving and growth in the number of both professional and amateur handweavers that varied and interesting yarns are now comparatively easy to procure. In the 1930s the supply was so limited and uninspiring that ideas for design were perpetually frustrated. I was becoming increasingly absorbed in the weaving of furnishing fabrics, and that was the time when varied texture and effect yarns were first being produced. Yarn manufacturers were making slubs, bouclés, knops, gimps, and the like, and man-made fibers were outgrowing the early "artificial silk" phase and taking on a life of their own. It is odd to think back to a time when spun rayon appeared as an exciting and desirable new yarn. I was keen to get my hands on these new threads and experiment with their use and the only way to do so seemed to be through a formation of some link with the furnishing textile industry.

Work for Warner and Sons
About this time I formed a friendship with Alec Hunter, the manager of the Braintree Mill of Warner and Sons, Ltd. This firm had a long and interesting history. Formerly a part of the old Spitalfields silk industry in the East End of London, they had subsequently moved from London to Braintree in Essex, continuing to produce exquisite and elaborate silk fabrics: damasks and brocades, satins and velvets, mainly on hand-operated Jacquard looms. They were all traditional in design. Some years before I met Alec Hunter, a new department was started under his auspices for the machine production of furnishing fabrics. These were modern in design and in strong contrast to the long-established silk weaving. The success of this new department helped the firm to survive the economic depression of the 1930s. Alec was a rare combination of artist and businessman. His father, Edmund Hunter, had managed a small family business, designing and producing fine and unique woven textiles, mainly on Jacquard looms. Looking at these fabrics, one was aware that this firm had its roots in the beliefs and idealism of William Morris. Although Alec was an artist of his own time and a fine modern designer, the influence of his home environment was strongly present in his outlook and personality.

I was attracted to Warners by this mixture of old and new, and I suggested to Alec Hunter that I might be taken into the business to produce exclusive handwoven furnishing fabrics. To my extreme delight and, I may add, surprise, he and the Managing Director agreed. In great excitement I traveled down to Braintree from London, expecting to find a grim and gaunt mill building such as I had grown accustomed to during my Yorkshire childhood. I was happy to find a pleasant old two-story mill, built of brick and white weatherboarding and looking welcoming and not at all intimidating. Here I found wonderful opportunities and great happiness. In those days I used to bicycle to work and often in the evening after I had been home I would go out again and ride round the mill, just for the pleasure of seeing it and thinking of my work there.

14

The contrasts in production and activities at Warners were most interesting. In the large room where I and my two assistants were weaving heavily textured fabrics with yarns which would hardly run from the shuttles, Lily Lee was weaving, by hand, silk velvet in crimson and purple for the peers' robes to be worn at the coronation of King George VI. She went doggedly on weaving, hour after hour and day after day, on the long warps, inserting the fine-grooved wires to lift the pile warp and cutting the silk where it passed over each groove with a specially constructed, razor-sharp knife to form the exquisitely fine silk pile. Absorbed as I was in my modern fabrics, I failed to learn as much as I might have done from the fine craftsmen in silk weaving who were working all around me, but a certain amount must have rubbed off and made me aware that handweaving *could* be concerned with fine as well as heavy threads. I found out that power looms could not handle the finest threads and closest counts and that beyond a certain point the fabrics had to be handwoven. This weaving was men's work. The heavy treadles lifting the Jacquard machines could not be operated by women. Cheerful Bill Beard taught me to "twist-in" a new silk warp to an old one with perhaps three or four hundred ends per inch. He spent most of his life doing just this. I believe that I and my work were a source of some surprise and amusement to these people. I remember "Old Walter," one of the firm's senior handweavers and a superb craftsman, could not get over his amazement at the variety of designs that I produced on a four-harness loom. These weavers were of a different caliber from those I had been associated with at art school and at Heals.

The Outbreak of War

My work for Warners was, however, doomed to failure, for the years were those just preceding the outbreak of war. Just as the new department was getting on to its feet, the blow struck and in 1940 I left the firm for, as it turned out, a strange miscellany of occupations concerned with the war effort.

Looking back to the years of the Second World War it is surprising to recall how much of the time one spent simply being bored. At the outset we tried to prepare ourselves for danger, bereavement, pain, horror, and enemy invasion. Many of these hazards we faced, though by almost a miracle we in Britain were spared the last of them, but the unexpected and recurring pattern that linked them was boredom. Hours and hours in air-raid shelters, night after night of fire-watching, months of compulsory employment in uncongenial jobs where at best one was sufficiently busy to make the days go reasonably quickly and at worst one had not enough to do, and that was the most boring fate of all. Of course, there were some highlights, new friendships and relationships with diverse people and occasionally work that at any rate *seemed* at the time to be immensely vital and worthwhile. For me, one such experience was outstanding.

Weaving at the Courtauld Institute of Art

At the start of the war the Courtauld Institute of Art vacated its premises in Portman Square, London. Professor D. V. Thompson, of the Department of the History of the Technology of Art, had, however, obtained permission to use his laboratories in the building for research in connection with the Ministry of Aircraft Production. This small unit was concerned, among other things, with designing a special camera, and this required an exceptionally flexible and opaque shutter fabric. I was slightly acquainted with Professor Thompson and, remembering me and my knowledge of weaving, he conceived the idea of bringing me into the research unit to design a suitable fabric. Here indeed was excitement and opportunity and I leapt at the chance. Abandoning, at short notice, a routine job in a drawing office, I plunged into this new and exciting work, proud to think that even a handweaver could, as I thought, make a significant contribution to the war effort.

A loom was set up in Portman Square, fine filament rayon yarns from Courtaulds were supplied, and I worked long hours for many happy months, returning to my flat in the blackout with the sirens wailing, the guns firing, and distant bombs falling. In addition to the camera shutter fabric, I was instructed to try my hand at other jobs and even assisted Professor Thompson in designing a space suit for astronauts! Believe it or not, we actually dressed up an artists' lay figure in a miniature suit and showed it proudly to the Ministry of Aircraft Production. I need hardly add that they were *not* interested. As for the shutter fabric, when it was completed it was pronounced very satisfactory, but in the meantime the Ministry had procured some other fabric which, though not so good as ours, was considered adequate and less expensive to produce. So eventually the job petered out and the time came to move on again. Though completely futile as it turned out, it had at least given me vast interest and entertainment for many months and the new experience of weaving with the finest possible threads and with warps around six hundred ends per inch.

Work for the Cotton Control

The work that followed this drew me down to the utmost frustration and boredom. As I sat at a desk in a Government department with almost nothing to do, the slow hours passed, while I shivered in an inadequately heated room (this was late in the war and fuel was very scarce) and surveyed the brown linoleum on the floor. There was another vacant desk in the large bleak room and one morning I came in to find a real, live man seated at it. Having too little to occupy me, the powers that be must have decided that I needed assistance. He turned out to be a hatter — depressingly sane, alas! I regarded him with the limited appreciation the prisoner in solitary confinement affords to his pet rat. No doubt his feelings for me were reciprocal.

At last this penance terminated. It was the autumn of 1943, not much more than eighteen months before the end of the war, but this was a time of great depression and darkness. Women as well as men were drafted to various forms of employment, and I wondered with a good deal of anxiety what would happen next. What, in fact, did happen was an experience that I always think of in terms of emerging from a long and dark tunnel into brilliant and glorious daylight.

The Council for the Encouragement of Music and the Arts

The present Arts Council of Great Britain grew from an earlier organization known as the Council for the Encouragement of Music and the Arts, or CEMA. This body, under the Chairmanship of Lord Keynes and the Secretaryship of Mary Glasgow, was set up in the war with the object of providing cultural entertainment and enjoyment for the wartime population, often uprooted from their homes and living in unfamiliar parts of the country, many working long, hard hours in factories. Under the directorship of a London headquarters, a number of regional offices were set up covering the whole country, and I had the immense good fortune of being appointed as Assistant Regional Director in the Yorkshire Region, with its office in Leeds.

This appointment brought me back to my home ground and I had the pleasure of returning to a place where I still had friends and contacts and was close to a familiar and deeply loved countryside. Under the leadership of Douglas Fayers we were a small but enthusiastic group at our Leeds office, and we worked hard and long hours at a task that seemed supremely worthwhile. I was in charge of the art section, and I confess now that I largely learned as I went along, though I did not admit to this at the time. Fortunately my zest for the job made up for a good deal of ignorance. Nowadays the art assistants in the Arts Council have University degrees in the fine arts but not so then. Most of my work consisted of finding suitable places where art exhibitions could be shown. These exhibitions were usually assembled in London and circulated throughout the country, though sometimes we had the pleasure of creating shows in our own regions. They ranged from minor collections, often of reproductions, to original works of some importance. Traveling round Yorkshire to art galleries, libraries, schools and colleges, and any other public building that could house a small art exhibition, I made many friends and learned a lot about people as well as about art. All this seemed a far cry from weaving, and I sometimes wondered if I should ever return to my chosen occupation, but in all this time I was enlarging my knowledge of the arts — not only painting and sculpture but music and drama, with which I was indirectly concerned. True, my involvement with musicians often consisted in doing duty at factory lunch-time concerts — unpredictable occasions when pianos and prima donnas were often precariously balanced on loading platforms, and vicious electric bells, calling all back to work after the lunch break, were quite capable of going off suddenly just at the climax of some tenor's impassioned rendering of Samuel Coleridge-Taylor's "Onaway, Awake Beloved." It could happen that enthusiasm, tact, and good humor stood us in better stead than knowledge of the subject. And I learned so much — I can never be sufficiently grateful for the chance to meet artists and become intimate with their works, to hang exhibitions, to talk to lecturers and mix in the art world at a time when communication was easy and the barriers of intellectual snobbery were down.

The few years after the end of hostilities proved a very rich time for us in Britain to see a number of great works of art from European collections. Most of these had been hidden away underground during the war, and before they were returned to their permanent settings many of them went on tour. At one time the National Gallery and the Tate Gallery were showing concurrently masterpieces from galleries in Munich and Vienna. The impact of these two magnificent exhibitions was overwhelming. I shall never forget a room in the Tate where four Rembrandt self-portraits in a row regarded the crowds of spectators with eyes of infinite sadness and infinite wisdom. In 1947 a fine collection of French tapestries was shown at the Victoria and Albert Museum. There I first discovered the splendid Apocalypse series from Angers, which subsequently led me to that city on a memorable pilgrimage.

All the rich and varied experiences of nine years' work with the Arts Council were hard to relinquish but the time seemed ripe to consider a change. A chance encounter with an old friend got me the loan of a studio in Leeds where I could set up my looms again, and gradually I was drawn back until I decided that the time had come to make a complete break and try my luck again as a full-time free-lance weaver.

Free-Lance Weaving — Phase Two

The period that followed was a difficult one. It was now eight years after the war, and I had been away from weaving for thirteen years, except for the brief spell at the Courtauld Institute. I faced the prospect of reintegrating myself in the textile world from a cold start, but the intervening years had enlarged my outlook, vastly increased my understanding and appreciation of the arts, and imposed standards that were perpetually challenging. I had also acquired an interest in working with fine yarns.

I tried my hand at designing for industry, besides weaving individual pieces, but this was never successful, although it helped me financially at a difficult time. Eventually it became clear that specialization in my own technique and design concepts was the right path to take. The extension in design possibilities that arose from my early experiments in inlay, using a fine tie-down warp, at first plunged me out of my depth as a designer and I asked Austin Wright, a well-known British sculptor and a friend of mine, if he would be interested in collaborating with me in my experiments. He willingly agreed, producing drawings which I interpreted freely in terms of weaving (see Figure 1-1, page 11). Looking back, it is perhaps interesting to recall that I turned to a sculptor rather than a painter for assistance, forecasting my enduring interest in sculptural forms as a source of inspiration.

A chance to collaborate on a Christmas crib for Wakefield Cathedral gave us the opportunity of working on a big scale, and a commission for two large hangings for the newly rebuilt Lady Chapel in Manchester Cathedral followed almost immediately. Again, the woven hangings were interpreted from drawings by Austin Wright.

A decision to move from Yorkshire to the Gloucestershire cottage where I now live made this collaboration more difficult and I decided, with many doubts and hesitations, to attempt designing my own hangings. Austin Wright's help and influence had given me an invaluable start and from this point onwards I learned, with difficulty, to stand on my own feet.

My further experiences are embodied in the subsequent chapters of this book, but I cannot end this section without some mention of the stimulus and help that has come to me in recent years from my teaching work on both sides of the Atlantic. This has always been sporadic, taking the form of concentrated short courses or single lectures and demonstrations, and I find this suits the demands of my creative work better than any form of regular teaching. Not only does this work enable me to travel widely; it also introduces me to hosts of weavers, both professional and amateur, and affords opportunities of seeing their work and exchanging ideas.

My own convictions on these matters are summed up in the short quotation from Antoine de Saint-Exupéry on the title page of this book.

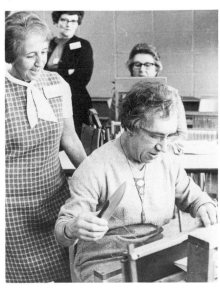

1-2. Teaching in New Jersey, 1970.

chapter 2

THE MOORMAN TECHNIQUE

The technique to which my name has been given is so simple that I hesitate to claim it as a discovery. It has, however, dominated my work for the last twenty years. I still find a fascination in what can be produced by this method and am all the time developing it in new directions. I cannot think that I have stumbled on a unique or original cloth structure. Surely the archaeologists of Peru have at some time or other picked some cloth with exactly the same structure out of those treasure-laden desert sands? I am prepared to believe that it is used in some of the very many modern weaving studios in Scandinavia or, indeed, in any part of the world where the craft is practiced. Certainly I "invented" the weave, that is, worked it out by long and patient experiments until I arrived at the present cloth structure, but I know only too well how easy it is to discover for oneself something in common use. When I was little more than a student I "invented" leno weaving.

The desire to develop the technique under review stemmed from my early fascination with traditional tapestries. In my twenties I visited the Cluny Museum in Paris and was overwhelmed and enchanted by the "Lady and the Unicorn" series of tapestries. I also visited Norway and Sweden and the hangings I saw in these countries made a deep impression on me in a rather different way. While the French masterpieces have an almost magical splendor, calling up visions of the Age of Chivalry, the Scandinavian works seemed less remote and, in some ways, more inspiring because so much nearer to the sort of weaving I was working on at the time. I was, and indeed still am, fascinated with the problem of trying to express an artistic concept in terms of weaving, and at that time traditional tapestry seemed the only technique that would give me the scope I needed. Had I been born later, had I come under the influence of modern European trends, I might never have deviated from these traditional methods. As it was, I found it all too slow. *Surely* there must be some way of producing free pattern over the whole area in question by a less laborious method? Some form of inlaid wefts introduced into an overall background fabric seemed the only possible solution to the problem, but it was essential to achieve a density and richness of color and texture such as cannot be produced by ordinary inlay techniques. It appeared that two things had to happen. Firstly, the inlaid areas of color had to be bound down to the ground weave by a tie-down warp thread which was fine enough to be barely visible but strong enough to stand up to the strains to which it would be subjected. Secondly, the cloth structure must be designed so that the ground wefts, running from selvedge to selvedge, would lie at the back of the areas of inlay, somehow hidden away so that they did not break into the color areas but at the same time formed a solid cloth background.

I explored the problem in many ways, discovering several quite interesting and effective cloth structures as I went along, but none of them seemed the perfect answer. After quite a long experimental period I arrived at the cloth structure explained in detail in the following pages. This is the basic weave which, with its variations, I have used fairly constantly over the last twelve years and which has carried me through a great many changes and developments in style and design.

The Cloth Structure — What It Is
Figures 2-1 and 2-2 illustrate the basic cloth structure referred to. The first figure shows the cloth woven with an abnormally light beat so as to indicate exactly how the wefts follow each other in sequence. It will be seen that the heavy inlay weft here is sparse, with the lighter-toned ground weft visible between each inlay thread. Figure 2-2 is exactly the same weave beaten up normally. It will now be seen that the ground weft between the inlay threads has disappeared and the heavy inlay has slipped into its proper position under the fine dark tie-down warp and lies *on top* of the ground weft. This makes possible the production of solid areas of heavy inlay without cloth distortion. The dark tone and the fineness of the tie-down warp make it relatively inconspicuous when passing over any colored inlay. Thus, clarity and strength of color in the inlay can be achieved.

This very simple weave fulfils the two essential needs already mentioned. It has one other important attribute. Weavers who have worked by ordinary inlay methods will know that one quickly arrives at a "build-up" in the cloth structure so that the inlaid area gets distorted lengthwise, and it is necessary to insert some extra wefts in the nonpattern areas to compensate for the distortion. In the technique described, this does not occur, owing to the way the inlay slips down on top of the ground weft, rather than lying beyond it. I have found that it is possible to inlay really thick, multiple wefts by this method without overall cloth distortion.

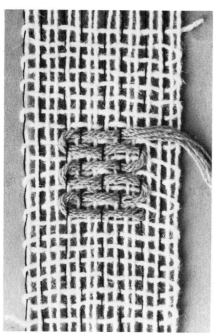

2-1. The basic cloth structure with weft lightly beaten to show cloth construction.

2-2. The basic cloth structure with weft naturally beaten.

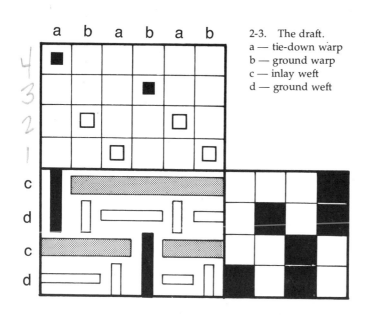

2-3.   The draft.
a — tie-down warp
b — ground warp
c — inlay weft
d — ground weft

The Cloth Structure — How It Is Made

The Loom
The cloth can be woven on a four-harness treadle loom of the jack or countermarch variety or on most four-harness table looms. It cannot easily be woven on a counterbalance loom, as it depends on a single lift of harnesses three and four. A loom with two warp beams is useful but not essential.

The Draft
The draft given in Figure 2-3 is exactly as used for the cloth shown in Figures 2-1 and 2-2. It is the draft I usually employ in my own weaving. The following specifications, however, are not as used in most of my hangings. They are given as a guide to the production of a sample or diagrammatic fabric, where clarity rather than subtlety is of prime importance.

In preparing the following directions for weaving samples and exploring some of the possibilities inherent in this technique, I have had in mind the importance of specifying both equipment and materials which are in common use among handweavers and fairly easy to obtain through normal channels. Any weaver who explores this technique and wishes to go further with its use will almost certainly take the trouble to obtain different and more subtle yarns which are exactly right for the project in view. This subject is dealt with in detail in a later section of this chapter (see page 33).

The Warps
The ground warp is 2/10 cotton, light color, twenty-four ends per inch; the tie-down warp is 2/20 cotton, dark color, twelve ends per inch. These warps (thirty-six ends per inch in all) may be warped and rolled on separately where two warp beams are available or may be wound as one warp. The warps being threaded through the harnesses in accordance with the draft (Figure 2-3), they are entered in a twelve-to-the-inch reed with three ends (two light and one dark) in each dent.

It should be noted that these specifications as to size of yarns and dentage of reed are only approximate. If yarns and reeds of other near sizes are more easily obtainable, it is quite in order to use them for sampling purposes.

As the ground and tie-down warps are used independently and at different tensions, it is wise to use two warp beams if these are available. When this is impossible they can be united in one warp in the ratio of two thick light ends to one thin dark end. If this has been done it is possible that one or other of the warps may slacken as weaving proceeds and in this case it will be necessary to devise some means of tensioning the slack warp. A weighted rod inserted in the slack threads will usually correct the fault, or wedges of paper or other suitable material can be used around the warp beam.

Selection of Warp Threads

The selection of threads for both ground and tie-down warps is a matter of great importance. For first experiments and for discovering some of the potentialities of the technique, the two cotton warps specified above and prepared as either one or two units are suitable. As comparatively few looms have two warp beams, it is wise to avoid as far as possible the tension problems which are apt to arise when two different threads, often composed of different fibers, are used in a single warp and are subsequently fulfilling different functions in the production of the cloth. A look back to Figures 2-1 and 2-2 will show that this is the case in the weave in question. The tie-down warp is subjected to a good deal of strain, and this strain is unevenly spread over the cloth surface. It therefore needs to be composed of a yarn that has three qualities: *fineness* in order that it will be inconspicuous, *strength* in order that it will stand up to the strains to which it will be subjected, and *elasticity* in order that it can both give and take as it is used to tie down the varied textures and bulk of the inlaid areas. Of the natural fibers I believe cotton to be the most suitable — linen lacks elasticity, and wool in extremely fine counts lacks the necessary strength. Silk appears to have all the necessary qualities but is less durable than cotton and is apt to perish in strong sunlight. Of the man-made fibers there are doubtless many suitable fine threads being produced, but these are not always easy for handweavers to obtain. Nylon monofilament is often suggested to me as an ideal yarn for the purpose, but the extreme difficulty in handling it seems to me to be a great disadvantage. If, then, a cotton tie-down thread is selected, it is wise to use a cotton ground warp also, especially if a single warp beam is used.

The structure of the loom that is available is also a determining factor in the selection of yarns. If similar warps are set up on two different looms, it often happens that one will weave easily and smoothly whereas the other will cause constant trouble. A weakness in the design of many looms is the lack of adequate distance between the front and back of the loom. The shorter the distance, the greater the strain that is put on the warp threads as the heddles lift them to form the shed. Small table looms, in particular, are at fault in this way. At the end of this chapter are comments on loom design with special reference to the technique in question.

Weaving the Samples

However much the weaver may deviate at a later stage from the following exercises he will, I believe, find it useful to have a set of samples to refer to. In providing instructions for six exercises, I have tried to cover, in progression, the main potentialities of this cloth structure without being sidetracked into the many and varied design opportunities that may arise from a practice and study of these basic design elements.

The following points apply in weaving the samples.

1) Plain areas. Where inlay is introduced, an inch or two of plain weave (Exercise 1) should be woven before starting the instructions for inlay; similarly at the end of the sample and, where appropriate, between isolated areas of inlay.

2) Selvedges. A special selvedge, differing in drafting or entry in the reed, is unnecessary, but it is helpful to tie the first and last quarter-inch section of the warp considerably tighter than the main section. This provides taut edges.

3) Displaying samples. A group of samples is easier to examine and assess if each one is mounted on paper or cardboard and looked at as a separate entity instead of being woven as one long sample, where one design often detracts from the appearance of its neighbor. It is wise, therefore, to set up a warp long enough to leave unwoven gaps of at least one inch between the different exercises. An easy way of doing this is to insert a number of one-inch-wide strips of firm paper or cardboard into the warp between the samples. When the complete work is cut off the loom, these strips can be withdrawn and the different samples detached from each other and suitably mounted. Remember that they will look much better if they are pressed with an iron before mounting. A collection of samples that pleases the eye as well as giving useful information is a great step in the direction of good designing.

4) Wefts. In the instructions given, the different wefts are indicated by numbers:

1 denotes the main structural ground weft.

2 denotes the additional decorative ground weft.

3 denotes the inlaid weft. This may be a single yarn or a variety of yarns. The different varieties are labeled 3a, 3b, 3c, etc.

5) Warp tension. Although the tie-down warp is remarkably accommodating as regards tension, it is advisable to avoid too much concentration of heavy inlay in one area. For example, if a heavy, central, vertical stripe were woven, it would be found that the center tie-down threads would tend to become tight, and the outside threads would slacken. Without laying down any rule, it is wise to distribute inlaid areas as widely as possible.

6) Inlay shuttles. These may be of various types. Small boat shuttles, small stick shuttles, netting shuttles, and many others are used for inlay and weavers have their own preferences. Alternately, threads can be wound into butterflies.

Exercise 1 — Plain Weave

It will be realized that some form of ground weave is always present and nearly always visible in some area of the finished fabric. This is formed by a single thread running from selvedge to selvedge, creating a plain weave. In areas where inlay appears, this same weft continues to form the ground between each insertion of an inlay or group of inlays. The selection of the right ground weft for the work is most important. Fiber, texture, color, and size should all be carefully considered, and it is advisable to experiment with a variety of yarns before starting on a project.

To obtain a suitable ground weave, the size of the ground weft should be not less than the 2/10 cotton suggested for the ground warp.

As weaving of this plain ground proceeds, a rather irregular effect may appear, sometimes suggesting a threading fault. This is caused by the dark tie-down warp end moving erratically to the wrong side of its neighboring light ground warp. A close look at Figures 2-1 and 2-2 (page 22) will show how this can happen when three warps (two light and one dark) travel through the same dent in the reed. By varying the size of the reed or the grouping of the warp threads in the reed, or both, this problem can be overcome, and a number of variations are set out below (page 35).

Harnesses raised	Weft
1 & 3	1
2 & 4	1

2-4. Exercise 1 — weaving chart.

Exercise 2 — Plain Weave with Additional Ground Weft

The ground weave can sometimes be enhanced by the introduction of a second ground weft in a *fine* yarn. This second weft usually looks best when inserted in a ratio of two basic ground wefts to one additional ground weft. For this second weft, a fine bouclé or gimp, a fine filament rayon or a subtle contrast of color are suggested.

Harnesses raised	Weft
1 & 3	1
2 & 4	1
4	2

2-5. Exercise 2 — weaving chart.

Introduction of Inlay

Exercises 1 and 2 are introductory to the true use of the technique. Exercises 3 through 6 explain some of the varied pattern effects which can now be produced.

By studying the illustrations accompanying these exercises it will be apparent that areas of inlay may be introduced in a variety of ways: as isolated shapes within the fabric area giving a sparse or scattered pattern effect (Exercise 3); adjacently to form a solid pattern, with the ground weave completely hidden, giving an effect similar to traditional tapestry (Exercise 4); as overlapping areas of transparent color or value (Exercise 5); and as both transparent and heavily textured areas, with varied yarns, both thin and thick, smooth and rough, inlaid in the same shed (Exercise 6).

As soon as weaving these exercises proceeds, a problem will arise concerning the running in or "losing" of the cut ends of the inlaid wefts at the start and end of a pattern area. A section at the end of the chapter (page 35) deals with this matter.

Exercise 3 — Isolated Shapes Inlaid

The interest here is in the variety of yarns used as inlay. Heavy straight yarns can produce a solid and flat effect. Heavy effect yarns, such as

2-6. Exercise 3 — isolated shapes inlaid using varied yarns.

bouclés and looped mohair, can produce a solid rough-textured effect. Fine straight yarns can produce a shadowy effect with the ground weave showing through. Fine effect yarns can produce a speckled appearance. The directions in Exercise 3 are for inlay on a *plain* ground weave, as in Exercise 1. (A different and more textured cloth can be produced by inlaying on the ground shown in Exercise 2.)

Note that the inlaid shapes here are rectangular. This is an easy shape to weave and so makes a good starting point for understanding the technique. Later exercises use other more complex shapes.

It is interesting to try the variation shown in Figure 2-8 and note the different effects which occur.

Harnesses raised	Wefts
1 & 3	1
(3) *tie down*	(3 inlaid)
2 & 4	1
(4) *tie down*	3 *inlaid*

2-7. Exercise 3 — weaving chart.

Harnesses raised	Wefts
1 & 3	1
3	2
3	3
2 & 4	1
4	3

2-8. Variation on Exercise 3 — weaving chart.

Exercise 4 — Inlaid Areas Adjacent

This produces an effect similar to traditional tapestry.

Basically this is the same cloth structure as in Exercise 3 and therefore the same weaving directions apply. To produce an effect similar to that shown in the illustration, the weaver will start with a single heavy inlay weft. This should be at least three times the weight of the ground weft (1), as it must completely cover the ground weave. A soft stranded yarn (two or three ends of a soft singles wool) will give a good covering effect. This inlay will run from selvedge to selvedge. When the area from the start to the base of the circle has been woven, two more inlay wefts must be introduced, one, in a different color, to form the circle, and another to form the ground area to the left of the circle. At this point it is useful to adopt a rule for weaving whereby the inlay threads passing under the tie-down threads lifted by harness 3 move from right to left and the same threads passing under harness 4 move from left to right.

The use of this technique to produce an "imitation tapestry" effect is of questionable value. Although my own work started from this concept, as explained previously, I have for a long time pursued other goals, allowing the technique to take over and lead the way to something unique and peculiar to itself. If, however, weavers wish to explore in this direction, it is

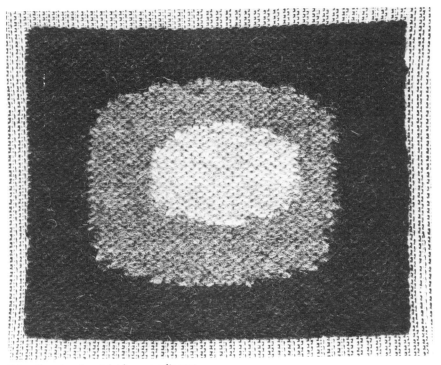

2-9. Exercise 4 — inlaid areas adjacent.

important that the inlaid areas in different colors should meet exactly. Without care it is easy to end up with either a tiny gap between inlaid areas where the ground weave is visible or a clumsy "ramp" where inlays overlap. (This is particularly noticeable when inlays meet on a vertical line.)

The correct join can be made in the following way. When two or more inlay threads are moving from right to left, under the appropriate tie-down threads controlled by harness 3, they start on the right and end on the left under *adjacent* ends in the tie-down warp. When they turn and move from left to right under threads controlled by harness 4, they *unite,* by passing under a common thread. It should be noted that on moving inlays from right to left the thread on the left moves first, that on the right follows (see Figure 2-10).

In weaving a diagonal or curved line between inlays the correct way is shown in Figure 2-11. The thread producing the increasing inlay travels for a short space in the same shed as the decreasing inlay, forming a double thickness of yarn for the appropriate length to follow the design. As the work proceeds, this double thickness will not be noticeable.

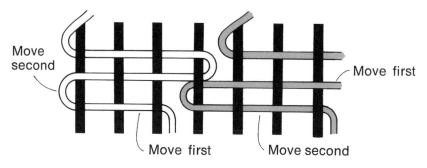

2-10.   Method of joining adjacent inlay. Vertical join.

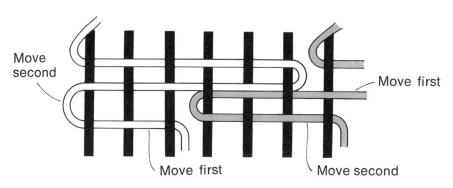

2-11.   Method of joining adjacent inlay. Diagonal join.

Exercise 6 — Varied Inlaid Yarns, Thick and Thin

This exercise is really the culmination of Exercises 1 through 5. It combines the introduction of heavy, textured yarns and fine yarns. We arrive at a fabric in which are incorporated the strong, positive statement derived from solid and vibrant areas of rich color and texture and also the elusive, shadowy effect inherent in Exercise 5. The order of harnesses raised and wefts is the same as shown for Exercise 5 but the inlay wefts 3a, 3b, 3c, etc. are considerably more varied and complex.

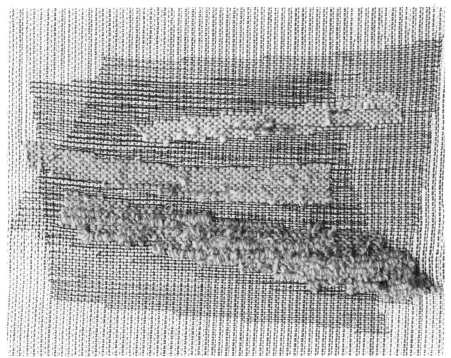

2-15.   Exercise 6 — varied inlay yarns, thick and thin.

Selection of Weft Yarns

In Exercise 1 I noted the importance of selecting the right ground weft for the work. The selection of inlay wefts is equally critical, and for experimental purposes it is helpful to get together a collection of varied yarns, both plain and effect threads, which can be freely drawn upon as work on the exercises proceeds. A collection of fairly fine yarns is useful, as these can be stranded (*not* plied) together. Sometimes stranding together quite a large number of fine threads gives plumpness and a covering quality that a heavy twisted thread lacks. In addition, the color variations that can arise from this method are very great.

A section of Chapter 5 refers in detail to the interrelation between fibers, textures, yarns, and colors, and the importance of their contribution to solving the problems of design.

Modifications in the Cloth Structure

The instructions given so far should in no sense be regarded as rigid. Within the basic principles of the technique it is possible and desirable to make modifications, according to the weaver's objective.

Modifications in Draft

The suggested warp for the basic exercises contains thirty-six ends per inch, of which twelve are tie-down warps. These operate alternately (six on harness 3 and six on harness 4). Thus the length of the float on the inlaid thread is one-sixth of an inch. This works out as a good average length, but fabrics put to different uses demand special consideration in determining the length of float that will be satisfactory. Generally speaking, a heavy yarn will tolerate a long float — a rug wool can successfully be floated for a half-inch or even more — whereas a fine yarn requires a shorter float. The visual and tactile effect of a float is a factor of prime importance. The long float gives richness and softness to a weave but diminishes toughness, crispness, and durability. A consideration of the qualities of a silk satin as compared to a silk taffeta composed of the same yarns exemplifies this point.

A wall hanging made from a rather delicate cloth structure will stand up to many years' wear, whereas the same fabric used as a cushion cover or a curtain material would be quite unsatisfactory. A careful assessment of the performance expected of the cloth will be the determining factor in deciding on the exact warp specifications.

The general effect of weaving Exercises 1 through 6 will be similar if any of the drafts in Figure 2-16 are used, although the ratio of ground warp to tie-down warp varies. The weaver must decide which draft is most suitable for his purpose.

2-16. Variations of the basic draft.
a — extra long inlay float
b — long inlay float
c — short inlay float

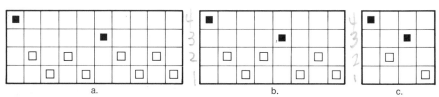

a.   b.   c.

Modifications in Sleying the Reed

The apparent fault in the ground weave mentioned on page 26 results from the neighboring ground and tie-down warps being entered in the same dent in the reed. This can be corrected in various ways:

1) If a 24-to-the-inch reed is available, the warp can be entered with two ground warps in the first dent and one tie-down warp in the second.

2) If a 12-to-the-inch reed is available, enter five ends (two ground, one tie-down, and two ground) in the first dent and one tie-down warp in the second.

If a 12-to-the-inch reed is used, the ground weave will show a slightly uneven effect such as is arrived at by using a spaced warp. This is often desirable and may be exaggerated in various ways. It is particularly useful in the production of a very light-weight and semitransparent ground weave. In many of my own works, where this sheer quality is stressed, I use very fine threads for both ground and tie-down warps and enter six ends in a dent (four ground, two tie-down). Using a 24 reed, I leave three empty dents between, so that my total number of warp ends is still thirty-six per inch. The fact that the warps are held close together in tight bunches in a fine reed sets up a resistance when the weft is beaten down. This results in a decided open space between wefts.

An exact specification of the cloth structure normally used in the production of my transparent hangings follows.

The ground warp is twenty-four ends per inch, 28 singles linen.

The tie-down warp is twelve ends per inch, 80/2 mercerized cotton (warps wound separately on two warp beams).

The ground weft is 16 singles linen, sixteen picks per inch.

Losing the End of the Inlaid Weft Thread

At the beginning and end of an area of inlay it will be necessary to lose the cut end of the thread by weaving it for a short length into the ground weave. This inlay thread should always be run into the ground weave shed *preceding* the first and the last inlay shed. Thus, if the inlay starts or ends at a point where harness 3 is raised, the end is lost in the shed formed by raising harnesses 1 and 3; if the inlay starts or ends at a point where harness 4 is raised, the end is lost in the shed formed by raising harnesses 2 and 4. The end must, of course, always be lost within the inlay area, not running outwards into the ground weave.

A neat way of starting a small inlay area, when a fairly short length of yarn will be adequate, is to work with a double thread. A single thread can be looped round the first tie-down warp in the inlaid area and the two ends brought together to form a single thread. If it is long enough, this can then be wound into a butterfly.

Loom Design

Technical details on the subject of looms would be out of place in this book, but in my teaching work I am often aware of the strains and frustrations put upon weavers in attempting to set up warps with fine yarns and counts simply because their looms are wrongly constructed. When I find that these strains are so great as to deter weavers from exploring further into the techniques that I have outlined in this chapter, I feel it necessary to make some comments.

If a weaver is setting up a warp with, say, thirty-six ends per inch, it is *essential* to be sitting in a relaxed and comfortable position when threading the heddles and the reed, otherwise fatigue and pains will quickly be induced by the unnatural strains on the body. Most small looms, and particularly table looms, impose unnecessary strains because the breast bar at the front of the loom cannot be removed during the threading process. Ideally it should be possible to sit, while threading the loom, in an upright position, close to the harnesses, and with the cross in the warp clearly visible without moving one's head and without exaggerated movements of the arms.

These points, of course, apply to threading *all* warps, but the problems quickly build up when one is involved with handling, say, nine hundred ends rather than three hundred. Looms vary in construction, and weavers thread up in different ways, but whatever the circumstances I suggest that some adaptations to existing looms are worth considering. Sometimes even the removal of a few screws will make all the difference between sorrow and joy.

chapter 3

VARIATIONS AND USES OF THE TECHNIQUE

Having carried out the exercises laid down in the previous chapter, the weaver will be starting to realize that he is only on the threshold of the explorations and experiments inherent in this technique. From this point on the way opens out and the problem of *how* to do it diminishes as that of *what* to do with it increases. We now find ourselves not at a given point on a straight road but at the center of a star with lines radiating in all directions. I have myself specialized in the use of this technique to produce tapestries and wall hangings, space dividers, and church textiles, but given the right incentive I could equally well have explored in different directions. It seems to me that this technique could be used interestingly in weaving dress fabrics and dress accessories, curtains, cushions, table linens, bedspreads, and even floor rugs. Nearly all these objects would pose a different problem in selection of yarns, ends per inch, and even modification of the basic draft as given on page 34.

Some Variations on the Exercises

The use of the technique to form a solid tapestry effect (Exercise 4) can be modified by leaving small areas of the ground weave visible between large, inlaid areas, which produces an interesting linear appearance. If a dark inlay is added to a light ground, it is possible, for instance, to produce the effect of a light corona around a dark object. Alternatively, a light inlay on a dark ground will give a dark and emphatic outline which can suggest the leaded strips separating and enhancing the brilliant colors of a stained-glass window (see Figure 4-3).

A build-up of light rectangles on a dark ground also suggests a different theme, as illustrated in Figure 3-4.

It will now be discovered that the ground weave can fulfil either a negative or a positive role in the design. It can be thought of as a background to positive areas of inlay: it often occupies the outer spaces of the entire work or flows between isolated inlaid areas. Here it has a negative quality — we are not strongly aware of it as we examine a work. If, however, it is used as described above to form a corona of light or piercing lines penetrating an inlaid area, it becomes a positive element in the design (see Figures 9-7 and 9-10).

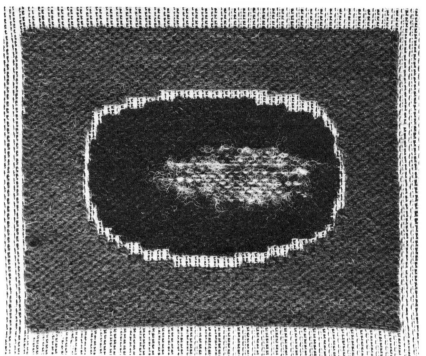

3-1. Solid inlay with light ground weave forming a corona effect.

3-2. "Blue Form." The corona effect used in a finished work.

3-3. "Chi-Ro." Solid inlay with the light ground weave used to form the symbol.

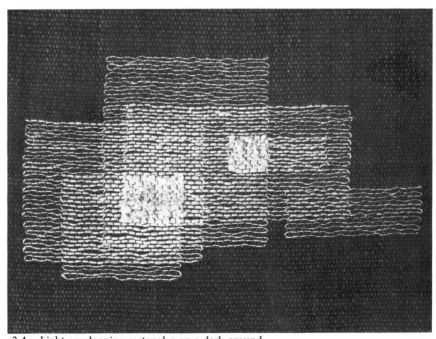

3-4. Light overlapping rectangles on a dark ground.

It is also interesting to see how an area of ground weave completely enclosed by a darker inlay assumes a heightened brightness. The enclosed light oval shape in Figure 3-5 is in fact exactly the same ground weave and therefore the same tonal value as the outside areas of the total work.

Sculptural or relief effects can be produced by a build-up of solid inlay, using looped or brushed mohair, heavy bouclés, chenilles or other heavily textured yarns, culminating in areas where the inlay yarns are looped round the tie-down threads or pulled out by hand to form a raised area. Introduction of some Ghiordes knots, as used in rug weaving, can give an interesting accent. A useful study is to see how many different textural effects can be produced by using a single inlay yarn in a uniform color in a variety of ways.

The looping technique referred to in Figures 3-7 and 3-8 can be used effectively to give an emphatic outline to a shape, as illustrated in Figure 3-9.

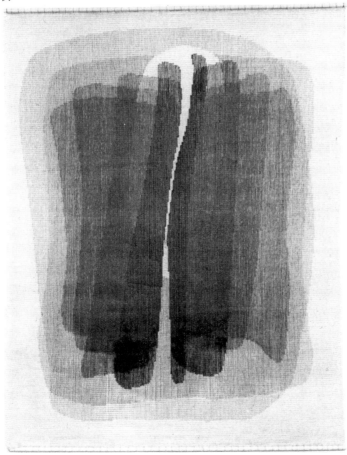

3-5. "The Gorge." The light ground weave emphasizes the central area.

3-6. Sculptural or relief effects.

3-7. Looping technique — method 1.

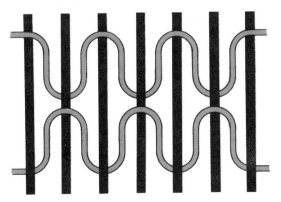

3-8. Looping technique — method 2.

An area of flat inlay can be enlivened by the introduction of a few strands of unspun wool, jute, or other interesting fibers. These can be drifted in, under the tie-down warps, alongside the regular inlay (see Figures 3-1 and 9-8).

A spaced warp such as that referred to on page 35 can be exaggerated to produce a useful and practical fabric, particularly suitable for a heavy curtain or space divider. By using a ground warp with twenty-four ends per inch sleyed in groups of eight threads in one dent at one-third-inch intervals and crossing it with a ground weft of two-ply wool with about twelve picks per inch, a fabric is obtained that is at once tough, semi-opaque, and quick to weave. This cloth structure was used for the two space dividers illustrated and discussed in Chapter 7 (see page 88).

Sometimes a designer feels a need to achieve an open space in a hanging — some point where the eye can penetrate right through the work. This can be a slit or series of slits. It can even be a hole, but the hole must not be so big that it weakens the cloth and the warp tension is lost.

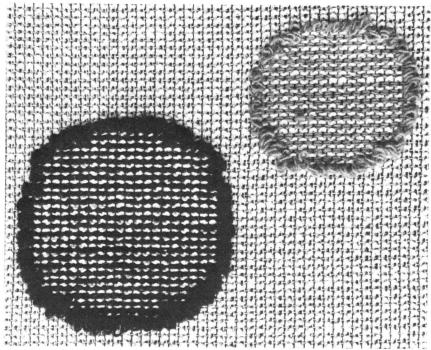

3-9. Looped outlines.

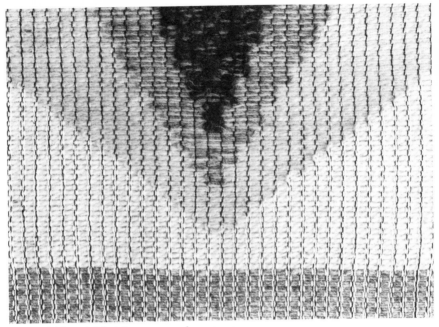

3-10. Thick and thin inlay on spaced warp.

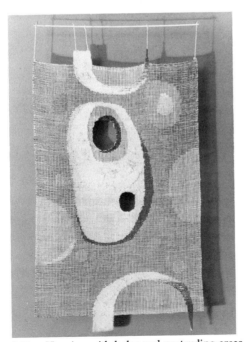

3-11. Hanging with holes and protruding areas.

Other variations on the Moorman technique can involve breaking away from the overall rectangle. A rectangle is the *natural* shape for a piece of weaving, and it is advisable to employ the natural and simple whenever possible. There is no virtue in being deliberately tortuous, but sometimes our design *needs* to include the unusual and unexpected. If we feel this need strongly enough, we are driven to devise some technical means of fulfilling it. We now move away from rules and directions and are compelled to devise methods that will give us the effects we desire.

By another, supplementary technique it is possible to divide the work at a given point into a number of sections, each of which is woven separately (Figures 3-12 and 3-13). These can be made to decrease in width so as to end up with a point. For this technique it is essential to set up a separate warp for each hanging.

The variations on the basic technique which have been examined and illustrated so far in this chapter are all in line with the original objective described at the beginning of Chapter 2 — that is, to produce a highly flexible cloth structure by means of which a wide variety of colors and

3-12. Divided hanging 1.

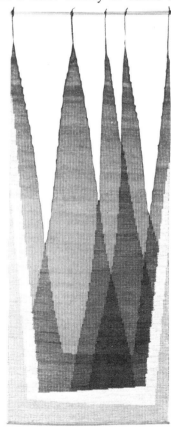

3-13. Divided hanging 2.

textures can be introduced in the form of inlay. It envisages the production of one-of-a-kind and decorative objects, usually wall hangings. The very fine and inconspicuous tie-down warp makes all this possible. In most cases it also makes possible the utilization of one warp (in fact, a ground warp and a tie-down warp working together) in the production of a variety of different pieces. If, however, we enlarge our scope to cover different works, particularly utilitarian objects such as furnishing fabrics and dress goods, we find that our "rules" may break down or need modification. For instance, we may be thinking of some fabric with an inlaid pattern, perhaps for a curtain fabric, where the color range is limited so that the tie-down warp, instead of being a negative, could become a positive element in the design. It could be made from a much heavier yarn in a distinct color and could match or blend with the overall color of the inlaid areas. The same idea might well apply to the design of dress fabrics, and here I believe there is much experimentation to be done. The possibilities are great and the field is wide open. Present fashion trends incorporate rich pattern areas to embellish a garment — borders, yokes, necklines, belts, sleeves, and many more, and the concept of the woven garment as a total design, as opposed to a length of dress material to be cut and stitched, is very much to the fore.

It should be remembered, however, that when the technique is geared to the production of functional fabrics, new practical points will emerge which were minimal or nonexistent when a purely decorative work was under review. We are involved with the performance of the fabric in use. Will it wash or dry clean? Will it stand up to constant movement and handling? Will it snarl or fluff up or sag or shrink? Will it have the required crispness or softness or draping qualities for its purpose? Can it be produced at sufficient speed to bring it within the price range of the customer? Some of these points are discussed in detail in Chapter 7 — "Commissioned Works, Problems and Opportunities." At present I only wish to draw attention to their importance and the necessary part they should play in the early stages of creating a design.

chapter 4

SOURCES OF INSPIRATION FOR DESIGNS

The preceding two chapters deal first with a technique and then with ways in which this technique can be used and sometimes adapted to satisfy some clearly defined aim. These two fields of study are only stepping-stones towards a final work. We have arrived at a point where we are impelled to come to grips with the problem of design. Although the subject of this book is weaving as an art form, I should regret any idea that we are only considering nonutilitarian objects such as tapestries and wall hangings and considering them, moreover, in a vacuum. All art must to some extent relate to its environment, and art, architecture, and the crafts are so closely linked that barriers and dividing lines between them must always break down. The fact that an artifact has a use, that it forms a necessary wall in a building or stops a draft or is a vessel for food or drink, does not preclude it from being a valid work of art. If we think of an oriental room with its considered proportions and spaces, the careful arrangement of the sparse contents, and the intellectual planning of color, we are not, I suggest, so very far away from an abstract painting by Josef Albers or Ben Nicholson. Thus, it is possible for a woven space divider or screen, a bed cover or group of cushions to be planned and produced as something with a more profound aesthetic content than is usually afforded to the design of a utilitarian object. Similarly it is possible for wearing apparel to be designed with so much artistry as to lift it almost into the field of mobile sculpture. It is a great mistake to downgrade useful objects, but unfortunately the buying public, while willing to pay good prices for wall hangings and tapestries, is averse to spending in a comparable way on usable woven objects. The regrettable outcome of this situation is the pressure on weavers to produce wall hangings when often their taste, skill, and artistic ability would find a better outlet elsewhere. It is here that the many weavers who are not pursuing their craft for a living — the amateurs in the true and dignified sense of the word, that is, those who love their art and practice it for love — are at an advantage. They have in their hands the chance to experiment at leisure and produce what they desire without counting the expenditure of time. Processes which are naturally slow, such as handspinning and natural dyeing, are not ruled out.

My own work, outside the area of my larger commissions, has been chiefly concerned with the production of wall hangings, and for the most part I have worked within the technique explained in Chapter 2. It follows that my thoughts on design have been geared to this specialized production. I hope that I have already made clear my respect for other techniques and objectives and that some of my thoughts on art and design will have a general application to many forms of textile art.

A design concept for a piece of weaving seems to me to derive from two main sources. On the one side we have the physical content of the work, that is, the materials, the equipment, and the techniques available. Coupled with these is the practical objective or use for which the article is intended. On the other side, we have the mental and emotional content, the spark which lights up and brings to life the physical content. I think of these as two converging streams. It is at the point where they mingle and become a river that the design in its entirety comes to life in the mind of the weaver. I recognize as an event of immense importance the rare occasion when these two elements, in meeting and merging, form a perfect synthesis. It could almost be referred to as a moment of truth. So frequently the result is off-balance and the two elements are in conflict. It can happen that our response to the materials and technique is so strong that the mental image, the thing that we have seen and wish to express in terms of weaving, gets distorted and crowded out. Alternatively, the image may be too strong and we may strain our technique beyond the limits that it will rightly tolerate.

To obtain the full value from this merging of the two sources, it is vital that each should be examined in detail and with equal respect, but before we look at these separately there are some points of general importance in considering design problems which it may be helpful to raise here:

Woven threads will never produce an elegant linear pattern such as a pen or pencil can create. The edges of forms will always have a rough and slightly fretted quality.

The most elementary and most natural design that arises from weaving is rectangular. Warp and weft intersect at right angles, and the first patterns we produce when we learn weaving are likely to be stripes and checks.

Weaving by means of inlay or tapestry techniques is a time-consuming process, and the complexity of the work increases steeply in relation to the number of different wefts inserted horizontally. We may be dedicated craftsmen with immense patience, but if we are involved with inlaying simultaneously more than about eight separate threads across a warp we reach a stage where everything becomes too frustrating and tortuous. Where possible we should aim to simplify.

The Physical Content of a Design

Weavers are particularly fortunate in that the materials of their craft are in themselves beautiful to both sight and touch. Both unspun fibers and spun yarns are inspirational in themselves. Handspun threads have unique qualities and sensitivities which can be aesthetically enjoyed in their own right. Color applied to threads, both by natural and by synthetic dyestuffs, sets up a whole range of emotional responses and the subtleties of the same dyes applied to varying fibers are far-reaching. These responses, added to our weaving experience and our experiments in cloth structures, suggest, in their own right, ideas for designs.

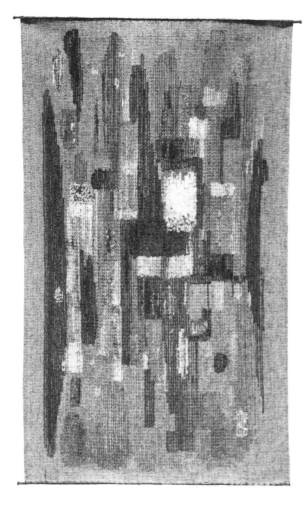

4-1. "Reflections in Water."

The Mental Content of a Design

Here we are considering the whole personality of the weaver. He is attempting to link some outside source of inspiration with that derived from the physical side of weaving, and he is aiming at a balance between these two elements. In looking for our outside source of inspiration we are concerned with vision and with the "seeing eye." This is something different from our normal way of observing our environment. Modern civilization binds us more and more closely to words. We use our eyes to recognize and *name* our surroundings by a sort of shorthand method. This seems to satisfy our normal wants, and our eyes pass on quickly to the next object. Walking in the country we say, "There is an ash tree, there an oak tree," but our eyes are lazy and we do not really *see* the trees as forms, patterns, and colors. I believe it is possible and most rewarding to ourselves, not only as designers but as a part of our daily lives, to foster and develop this "seeing eye." It takes time and patience. Sit for a time by a river and watch the reflections. Hold a steady eye on the surface of the water and really *see* the moving patterns and colors that are there before you. If you are a weaver and if you are impressed by the beauty of the patterns and colors, it is possible that they may lead your mind on to thinking in terms of woven design.

As our technical experience grows we recognize some design elements which seem valid for our own technique, and as our eye looks about for sources of inspiration our mind sets up a process of acceptance and rejection and we become more skillful at recognizing and embracing something that has not only inspired us but can also be expressed in terms of the technique at our disposal, a point which is examined further in Chapter 5. We are often aware of a tension between the physical and mental contents of our design. This tension may well bring a dramatic heightening to our thoughts but should not be carried too far.

If we now think back to our reflections in water, we find we possess, first, something which has inspired our vision and, second, a concept for a design which exploits some of the natural attributes of weaving, namely, rugged and imprecise linear patterns, a use of roughly horizontal and vertical lines, and the desirability of limiting technical complexity. These are the points referred to on page 47.

Looking at the woven hanging in Figure 4-1 the spectator might say, "But this is an abstract design. It could have been arrived at simply as an arrangement of woven shapes without any reference to water and reflections." I know that many weavers can and do design satisfactorily in a purely abstract way. I recognize and admire their work, but my own desire is to express and perhaps communicate something of my response to my environment through my craft. I am concerned with producing an abstraction from a visual experience rather than a true abstract. This abstraction can deviate so far from the original literal image as to be unrecognizable but still retain something of the primary vision and impulse.

4-2. "Tree Bark."

The danger in this line of approach is the temptation to strive for too literal an image and to arrive at something which will be strained and unhappy as a piece of weaving. In the course of my teaching I find that students lacking experience in this specific technique suggest designs that are too pictorial and complex and by forcing the technique beyond its proper limits are likely to fail in their objective.

At the start of my experiments in this technique I was tempted by the freedom which it offered to try for some design too close to my original sketch from nature and too far away from a woven fabric. I believe that a woven hanging should always show something of the unique qualities of the craft. An exhibition of works by Matisse included a very finely woven silk tapestry in traditional technique. It was so exact a replica of a painting by this artist that it was unrecognizable as a tapestry until one was standing so near as to make it impossible to see the object as a whole. This seemed to me to lessen equally the work of both the painter and the weaver. This is, however, cited as an individual case. The questions of designing for traditional tapestry, a subject with a long history and its own individual problems, lie outside the context of this book.

Our visual inspiration can be drawn from either nature or the creations of man. In contemplating natural objects we learn, as our experience grows, to select such patterns and forms as will lend themselves readily to our craft. Most people respond to the beauties of nature such as flowers, land- and seascapes, animals and birds. These may be valid sources of inspiration, but our problem is to extract from them some essential quality which does not depend on attributes that are in opposition to the natural demands of our technique. A flower may have design qualities quite outside its literal and linear pattern. The color, only, of a small wildflower embedded in a rock crevice and the overall shape of its leaves and stems may form the nucleus of a woven design (see "Herb Robert and Rock," Plate 3, page 83).

Alongside these time-honored and generally accepted objects of beauty there is a vast area of unexpected but significant form, color, and pattern all around us if we really search for it. Both artists and photographers of the present day use and record their visual experiences of subjects which may not immediately strike the casual observer as being worthy of attention. Rich rewards can come from the close study of small and isolated objects or groups of two or three objects — a fallen leaf on a pavement, a stain on a wall, a burning log, the strata of a rock formation, a few pebbles, the bark of a tree, three blades of grass.

Having selected our theme we then become involved in the process of abstraction and this is, I believe, something that can only be learned from our own personal experience, often involving long and patient experiment and study. It is a highly individual process and there are no set rules. A few tentative suggestions may, however, be helpful.

1) Any means we can adopt to break the habit of our normal and accepted vision and our pedestrian and everyday way of observing our environment can help us to sharpen our aesthetic insight. The shock of the unexpected can heighten our perception. If we lie on the ground, the landscape around us becomes something strange and different. If we turn our heads sideways, colors appear to intensify.

2) A deliberately blurred and out-of-focus image can be induced by regarding our object or scene through half-closed eyes. Irrelevant detail is eliminated, edges are softened, and we are nearer to the simplification that must always be our aim. Alternatively, if we take a close-up view of field flowers seen through blades of grass the image that emerges may surprise us.

3) A small rectangle cut out of a sheet of paper can be used as a frame to look through and isolate our subject. By forcing our eye to concentrate on a small section only of our total area of vision, we become aware of significant color and pattern which we might otherwise have ignored.

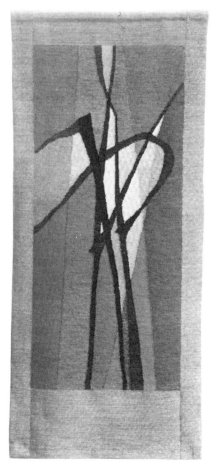

4-3. "Grasses."

4) A familiar object seen in a mirror can jolt and surprise our vision in a salutary way. We have probably all had the experience of seeing a well-known face reflected in a mirror and being surprised at how it differs from the accustomed image.

5) Close attention to the echoing shapes of shadows can be rewarding.

The temptation to use photographs as an aid to design is great. An ocean of photographic reproductions in both color and monochrome lies all around us, often recording just those unexpected views of our environment mentioned above. But, however these may appeal to us, it should be remembered that through them our vision is always reduced to something secondhand. The impact on our eye can never be as strong as when we observe the actual object. Although I look at and enjoy these collections of photographs, I seldom turn to them for a starting point for a design. The roughest of rough sketches, incomprehensible to anyone except myself, done, maybe, on the spur of the moment, on the back of an envelope or the spare page of the car handbook, helps me more than a photograph, even when referred to after a lapse of years, to re-create my first response to the thing seen and to provide a jumping-off ground for a design. When we try to record this response in the form of a sketch, we instinctively select the salient points and omit others which have no place in our theme.

Alongside this wealth of inspiration to be derived from our natural environment is another fountainhead from which we can draw for the enrichment of our creative ideas. I speak of the whole field of the arts. I have referred in a previous chapter to the enlargement of my life that came about through my years of work for the Arts Council and the privileges it brought me of associating with painters and sculptors and their works. The massive mountain range of the arts with its major peaks and its foothills is there for our exploration and for the enrichment of our life and thought. By subjecting ourselves to the powerful influences of those works of art which particularly move us, doors can be opened and new vistas stretch before us on the long road we travel in our search for a deeper understanding and mastery of our own craft. Sometimes a work of art can initiate a line of thought by which we as designers can get help in a specific way. We may compile a list of artists who help us and advance to meet us in much the same way as do the natural objects mentioned above. At other times the inspiration from the same artists may come to us in a subtler and more generalized way, as a heightening of our perception which may not result in an immediate or clear concept. The experts tell us that our subconscious mind goes on working for us below the level of our conscious awareness. Dr. Jacob Bronowski speaks of "the great iceberg of the mind." As a designer I am convinced that we can be helped in this indirect way. Moreover, the enrichment of our creative talents can stem not only from the visual arts; abstract images may be linked with an absorption in music and dance and our visual imagination may be sparked by a poetic concept.

In referring to a number of twentieth-century painters and sculptors from whose work I, personally, have derived help, and in showing reproductions of their art, I must stress that any idea of reproducing or copying such works in terms of weaving would be distasteful and impertinent. To draw on these works for inspiration is something quite different. Artists must always learn from each other and from previous generations of artists. Textile artists employ a different medium but their aims may have much in common, and to neglect any opportunity to draw on this rich reservoir can lead to a diminution rather than an increase in their stature.

The monochrome illustrations reproduced here can do little more than hint at a few aspects of the work of the artists in question, aspects such as might set in motion a fruitful line of thought in the mind of a textile artist. The choice is, of necessity, personal, and my decision to study these artists and their works as well as many others comes from an awareness that they are sending out signals to me that I wish to pick up and somehow incorporate in the process of thought that precedes the designing of a woven hanging. A designer wishing to lay himself open to such influences should, of course, study many works by the same artist, preferably in color and as far as possible originals rather than reproductions. From this observation certain principles have taken form in my mind which appear to me valid. I list them here as a starting-off point only. Beyond this point the way is open to us all to look and absorb according to our own choice and ability to respond.

1) The need for abstraction from an original theme. An evocative mood can penetrate a near-abstract work. In the works I have chosen by Klee, Bissier, and Moore this is clearly seen. Though they are nonrepresentational, we are left in no doubt as to the original theme from which they have taken shape. In the painting by William Scott the theme is less obvious but is still present.

2) The true and full use of the medium as a means of expression. Although this applies to all these works, we are particularly aware of it when we study the wood sculpture of Barbara Hepworth. The total form, with the open space at its heart, seems to be linked with immense subtlety to the patterns and rhythms created by the natural grain in the wood. In a completely different way Bissier's use of transparent paint is essential to the expression of his theme. In my own recent work I have been strongly influenced by what I have learned from a study of Bissier's tempera and watercolor paintings.

3) The depth and space that can be suggested through the subtleties and contrasts of texture. The painting by Klee, in particular, exemplifies this point.

4) The importance of the negative spaces and interludes both between the positive masses and surrounding them. Here we can learn much from Moore and Bissier.

4-4. Henry Moore, "Two Piece Reclining Figure." The Tate Gallery. Courtesy of the Artist.

4-5. Paul Klee, "The Castle Mountain of S." The Tate Gallery. Copyright SPADEM.

4-6. Ben Nicholson, "Tuscan Relief," 1967. The Tate Gallery.
Copyright Marlborough Fine Arts Ltd.

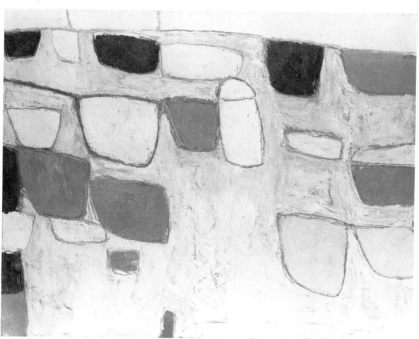

4-7. William Scott, "Ochre Painting." The Tate Gallery. Courtesy of the Artist.

4-8. Mark Rothko, "Light Red Over Black," 1957.
Copyright The Tate Gallery.

4-9. Julius Bissier. Courtesy of Frau Bissier. Copyright National
Galleries of Scotland. Photograph by Tom Scott.

5) The compelling power that can emanate from shapes of extreme simplicity. This seems to me to be something which can hardly be stressed too often as a goal for textile artists. Both Mark Rothko and Ben Nicholson can help us to understand how much a series of rectangles or near-rectangles can convey.

4-10. Barbara Hepworth, "Hollow Form with White." Copyright The Tate Gallery.

In addition to modern works of art such as I have suggested here and the host of other artists from whom we may learn, a wealth of inspiration is at our disposal from other man-made works spanning the centuries. Here are a few which have a strong impact on my thoughts: Stonehenge, Avebury, and other great prehistoric stone temples — I find these ancient standing stones with their strange anthropomorphic quality deeply moving and have used this theme many times in my work. Medieval and modern stained glass, Russian icons, with their immense richness of color and texture and the emphatic poses and gestures of the simplified human forms; oriental landscape and plant painting; the architecture of Manhattan. Our sources of inspiration surround us, on the shelves of our weaving rooms, in our houses, and in the cities and countryside. Our problem is to see, absorb, and use these gifts.

4-11.   Callenish Standing Stones, Isle of Lewis. Scottish Tourist Board.

4-12. "Standing Stones 1."

4-13. "Standing Stones 2."

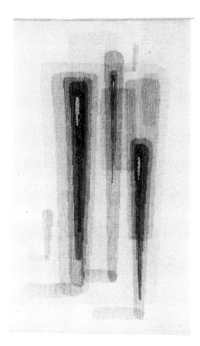

4-14. "Standing Stones 3."

4-15. "Manhattan."

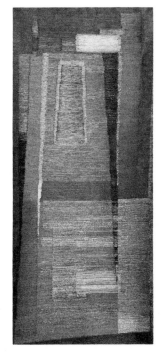

4-16. "The Corridor."

chapter 5

FURTHER POINTS ON DESIGN

It is unlikely that the success of a design will stand or fall on the results of a craftsman's theoretical studies. I believe that in these matters an inspired creativity will always take precedence over intellectual appraisal; probably we receive as a gift something more valuable than anything we can learn for ourselves. I know that in the course of my own work I leap before I look. The learning process follows the creative one. After the heat and excitement of production comes a period of cool assessment from which much can be learned. Points arise in the mind which start a train of thought, and it is some of these points that I want to consider in this chapter.

Scale

In addition to the obvious considerations of scale as it relates to the purpose and destination of a woven object, there is a different scale that is subtler but equally important. This is dictated by the cloth structure and the size and nature of the yarns to be used. A painting has no set scale of this kind — paint is not measurable. Weaving, however, starts with a group of threads of defined sizes and a cloth structure is formed consisting of a given number of ends per inch in both warp and weft. The relationship of these sizes and intervals to the dimensions of the finished work forms a part of our problem as textile designers, and we are aware that there is a right and satisfactory size for a hanging that depends on these given facts. If the same design is carried out on a larger or smaller scale, things are apt to go astray. The eye can be either over-aware or under-aware of the textural qualities of the work. This becomes plain when we weave on a narrow warp for sampling or experimental purposes and is a difficulty often faced by students attending short courses. The roughnesses and inequalities which are an inherent part of weaving stand out and catch the eye in an irritating way, whereas these same irregularities would only appear as lively, textured effects in a much larger work. Similarly, in my own technique, the fretted or stepped edge of an area of inlay that occurs when the shape increases or decreases may either look unpleasantly clumsy or be an asset to the design, depending on the scale of the work in question. On the other hand, if a really large work is envisaged, the textural qualities need to be overemphasized if a flat and uninteresting appearance is to be avoided (see "The Crucifixion," Plate 5, page 86).

On the whole I find small hangings particularly difficult to produce satisfactorily and have arrived at an approximate size which seems right for the technique and yarns employed. This, of course, is constantly open to change. As a guide I will add that my recent domestic-scale hangings are mainly thirty-eight inches high (the width of my loom) and twenty to thirty inches wide. This size seems to adapt to the yarns and technique in a satisfactory way.

The Pattern of Inlaid Areas

In the last chapter I referred to the importance of avoiding too great a complexity of design, and this particularly refers to the number of separate inlay threads to be introduced simultaneously into the weave. If you look at Figure 9-4 it will be clear that this design would have been impossible to weave if the warp had been vertical in relation to the finished work and the weft horizontal. If, on the other hand, the warp runs horizontally, the inlays are both limited to a manageable number and are also forming the comparatively wide areas that are desirable. Thus, it is possible to arrive at a design with a vertical movement without too lengthy and difficult a weaving process. Working in this way we are, of course, limiting the height of our finished hanging to the width of our loom. If we wish to produce a longer work, we are involved from the start in quite a different design problem.

In addition to avoiding a design that is too complex, it is important to consider carefully the nature of the shape we wish to weave in relation to our technique, remembering that a curved outline will never be a pure curve, a circle never an exact circle. Weave a group of clouds and they will look convincing, but add the moon and it will always look a bit clumsy. This leads us back to the point touched on in the last chapter, namely, the selection of the right subject matter to inspire our thought *in relation to the limitations of our craft.* Over a long period of trial and error I have found that certain objects now attract my eye in this way. Rough sketches of a few of these are shown (Figures 5-1 through 5-7).

These varied objects all have some things in common. In all of them the forms and patterns are clearly defined and in none are we involved with a symmetry so precise as to strain our medium beyond its proper limits. I regard all of them as valid sources of inspiration for my own weaving technique. There are of course many more.

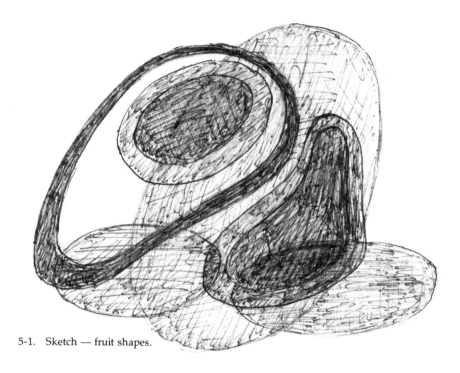

5-1.   Sketch — fruit shapes.

5-2.   Sketch — tree bark.

5-3.   Sketch — cliff formation.

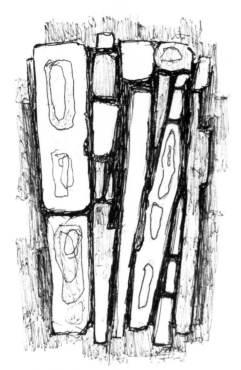

5-4. Sketch — rock strata.

5-5. Sketch — grasses.

5-6. Sketch — the trunk of a tree.

5-7. "Tree Trunk."

Fibers, Threads, and Colors

The interrelating qualities of fiber, thread, and color produce unique points for our consideration. Before the process of weaving there is the process of yarn preparation, and before this the raw materials must be selected. There are many of these and all have special qualities. Without becoming too involved in a scientific study of their properties, it is wise to arrive at some understanding of what they are and what they can offer us.

When these fibers are formed into yarns by a variety of processes our field of study enlarges to bewildering proportions and we are faced with almost an embarrassment of riches. Yarn itself can be a thing of beauty, even before it is woven, and it is interesting to devise cloth structures which allow the special qualities of the yarns to give the maximum of both visual and tactile pleasure — a spaced warp with a number of fine threads crowded together in the reed will resist the pressure of the batten so that the weft threads show individually instead of being crammed tightly together.

A fine dark weft woven in alternately with the heavier yarn (pick and pick) exaggerates the effect. If the heavier weft is a soft wool, silk, or cotton, the fabric woven will be very pliable, suggesting dress fabrics, but if a linen is used it is possible to arrive at a crisp, moderately firm fabric which is still light in weight and semitransparent.

The great diversity of yarns at our disposal calls for some restraint and can sometimes lead to disunity. There is something to be said for shunning many of the effect yarns and limiting ourselves to the use of high-quality straight yarns. If these are of fine counts they can be stranded together and by this means colors can be subtly blended. I have worked out a system whereby I can produce exactly the color I need for a work, and particularly for inlaid areas, without becoming involved in special dyeing. I have a complete range, approximating to a color circle, of intense primary and secondary colors in very fine cotton (I use 80/2 but slightly heavier yarns will do), that is, about twelve colors in all. To these are added two value ranges, one warm and one cool, from white to black and from beige to dark brown. These threads can be blended to produce other colors in much the same way that paint is blended. These fine threads can also be added to heavier yarns of different types to modify colors. It is an enormous help to a designer to have the freedom of a complete color range.

It is possible to produce handmade effect yarns in small quantities from straight yarns by various manipulative processes, and these can be extremely valuable in giving an accent of color or texture to other more restrained areas of inlay (see the altar frontal for Ripon Cathedral, Plate 4, page 86).

A very uninteresting three- or four-ply knitting wool can be brought to life by pulling on one strand of the group of plied singles yarns so that the others wrap around it in loose or tight bunches. The same idea can be used to give individuality to various texture yarns, most of which are constructed with a core thread. Find this thread and pull on it, and some interesting lengths of wrapped yarn will appear. Similarly, effect yarns can be created by twisting a group of straight yarns together by means of a spindle or other device. One yarn should be the core, and if this is drawn up the other yarns will wrap around it and interesting results can be achieved.

It is possible to produce many other handmade wefts. Chenilles and very narrow braids suggest new design openings. A crochet chain makes yet another interesting textured weft. Ingenuity of this sort both in color blending and in creating new textures can not only produce unique effects but also enable us to keep our stock of yarns within reasonable limits and still arrive at the precise colors and textures that we need.

It is important to remember the effect that the cloth structure and its texture will have on the final color. As soon as threads are woven, shadows are cast where they intersect. A piece of colored paper will not change as it is moved around, but a woven fabric will produce subtle differences as the light falls on it from different angles. A monochrome damask is an extreme example of this. The rich sheen of a satin weave is caused by the long silk floats reflecting the light.

It is interesting to consider the different effects that emanate from weaving with two yarns in complementary colors, that is, the colors lying opposite each other in the color circle — for example, green and red. When these two colors occupy fairly large and distinct areas so that the eye sees them individually, they intensify each other and seem to vibrate. If, however, they appear in much smaller units, perhaps woven with about twelve ends per inch in both warp and weft, the effect on the eye may be disconcerting, with an unpleasant friction between the two. But if they are woven in yarn so fine that the intersecting colors are blended by the eye, something quite different is seen. A muted color appears and we get a "shot" effect, which is something quite unique to textiles.

The response of different fibers to dyes poses some new problems. We find, for instance, that dyed linens have a slightly muted quality which may or may not be exactly the effect we need. If a brilliant dye is applied to both wool and mohair, the wool may appear bright and clear but the mohair will have an extra quality of intensity and brilliance.

Symbolism
Symbols have played an important part in the history of art. Church art in particular has amassed over the centuries an elaborate language of symbols, but most of these are now invalid. If we are designing an ecclesiastical work and want it to express something of the Christian faith, it is no good nowadays to incorporate fishes or ears of wheat in our design. The cross alone is universally recognized as a Christian symbol. The concept of symbols is, however, built into us through our history and it seems clear that

5-8. Varied handmade texture yarns.

many shapes, forms, and colors have special significance for us. Red, the color of blood and fire, spells danger. We are excited, alerted, alarmed. Blue conveys an idea of space. We speak of "going out into the blue." Yellow can mean light and hope, or green evoke the concept of growth and development. Even traffic controls make use of color symbols.

Similarly, shapes can evoke moods. An enclosed shape may make us feel safe and peaceful, whereas piercing shapes suggest action and dynamism. Contrast Figure 9-6 with Figure 9-10.

Numbers also can be evocative. A single form has an impersonal loneliness about it, whereas two forms relate to each other and adopt personalities that can quickly suggest humanity (see Figures 9-6 and 9-7). The number three has a quality which is unique, invoking ideas of magic and the fairy stories of childhood (three witches, three brothers, etc.).

I am not suggesting that we should make rigid rules for ourselves in these matters. Responses to colors and shapes will vary among individuals, and our instinct will probably serve us better than our brain, but I personally find much to interest me in thinking along these lines and believe that the outcome of my thoughts feeds the reservoir on which I draw in working out a design.

Happy Accidents

There is one last point on design to which I would like to draw attention. I refer to the occasional "gifts from the gods" that come our way and the importance of being on the alert for these and making full use of them. If our plans are too rigid it is only too easy to fail to recognize these when they appear. They can take many forms. They may come to us through our eyes or through our ears. Something we read, some remark we hear, some unexpected stimulus of nature, art, music, or poetry, some criticism or comment by a friend — all these things may heighten our perception and clarify our thoughts. Even the chance of an accidental piece of yarn in an unexpected color falling onto the cloth in the process of weaving may be the very thing to add life to our design. I think of all these things as bonuses. Our work will suffer if we fail to recognize and accept them and use them to the full.

chapter 6

BEGINNING AND ENDING PROCESSES

In addition to the main work on the loom, the production of wall hangings and many other woven objects includes two other activities. These could be described as the prelude and the finale. I refer to the practical production of the design and to the finishing and mounting processes which must be done after the work is off the loom. This chapter examines these two activities.

The Production of a Design

Methods of producing and working from a design are varied and if an attempt were made to specify exactly how it should be done most weavers would probably disagree. Some might even question the desirability of making any sketch or working drawing at all and prefer to let the design grow naturally from the process of weaving. The tradition of tapestry weaving over the centuries has, on the other hand, involved a full-scale cartoon prepared from a smaller drawing or painting. Between these two extremes lie many variants.

My own feeling is that some form of working drawing is necessary but that it should, if possible, be explicit without rigidity. I find it impossible to arrive at a finished product that has balance and rhythm without having worked out these attributes on paper before starting to weave. The essentials about which I need to be sure in advance are the arrangement of shapes within the total area, some idea of color (though this in my drawing may only be hinted at), and, most important, the proper balance of tonal values. Unlike most art forms, in weaving we are committed to the work as it grows. There is no going back; therefore our ideas need to be clear as to essentials at the start of the project.

Having said this, we must also consider the value of the unique contributory factors which flow into a piece of weaving through the technique and through the textures and colors we can create. As these appear under our hands in the course of weaving, we see something which we could not wholly envisage before the work started, and we may wish to modify our first ideas in the light of this new experience. It follows that our ideal working drawing, while containing the essentials mentioned in the preceding paragraph, will leave room for maneuver, particularly in the use of texture and color. Experience is, of course, invaluable. As we discover the effects of the colors and textures and design qualities which are inherent in our materials and techniques, our creative thoughts become increasingly geared to these discoveries and the seemingly slight sketches from which we work may, in fact, embody a clear and precise concept.

I have worked out a method which meets my own needs. Once again I put it forward as a suggestion rather than a rule.

In the last chapter I referred to the value I derive from the very rough and quick sketch, made at the special moment when I see and adopt my subject. These sketches may fill an immediate need or may not be used for months or years and are often filed away and forgotten. They contain, however, sparks of fire that can be fanned into a flame when they are needed. They are something entirely personal; they are rough, crude, and only intended to communicate back to me. Without being a good draftsman, I find I can produce these usable sketches provided I forget about precise drawing and allow pen or pencil to take control and record a thought or emotion. If I become self-conscious I am powerless.

The production of the working drawing from the sketch is, on the contrary, a deliberate process. The conputer of the brain has been working for us in the time between our feeding-in of the rough sketch and the moment when we are confronted by a white sheet of paper and a drawing board and need to produce a result. I still dread that moment and believe this feeling is shared by many artists and designers. The unsullied purity of the sheet of paper screams at us not to violate its virginity — the first stroke of the pencil feels like a crime! Nonetheless it must be made, and once we become involved in our problems we fortunately recover from our first inhibitions. We are now involved in abstracting, analyzing, introducing balance and rhythms, but still trying to incorporate something of our first source of inspiration in the design. I try to draw in a way that allows me as much fluidity and license as possible. Rather than working to a predetermined scale which would involve the production of a design within the confines of a rectangular shape, I fit my scale to my design when the drawing is finished. This method allows me to start the drawing at the focal point, usually somewhere within the central area of the total rectangle, and I let patterns flow out from this point until a totality emerges. Finally I indicate the enclosing rectangle. The drawing may be quite small, sometimes only a few inches across. I usually employ a ballpoint pen and either oil pastels or wax crayons. I find that these coloring agents suggest the blended colors and the textures of the weave more convincingly than paint. There is no question of producing a full-size cartoon, and the method employed in traditional tapestry weaving — tracing the design from a cartoon onto the warp threads — is not applicable to my technique. My small drawing is squared up to fit the width of my warp and pinned up on the loom in front of me so that I can constantly refer to it and check measurements and the positions of my inlaid areas. It must be remembered that while the width of our work will remain fairly much as it is when we are weaving, the length will contract considerably when the work is off the loom and no longer under tension. Only experience can determine exactly how much we lose lengthwise, but I find one inch in twelve is the least I dare allow. This means that either my drawing or my weaving must be elongated to avoid distortion of the design when the cloth retracts.

Weaving from a drawing in this way requires some experience, and here, once more, the need for simplicity is stressed. It is easy enough to draw a curved line with a pen, but it may be very difficult to follow that curve in weaving. It is sometimes a help to cut out in paper a shape to be woven and use this frequently for comparison with the shape forming on the loom.

The rather different problem of producing a design for a commissioned work is examined in Chapter 7.

6-1. Rough sketch for "Trees in The Wind."

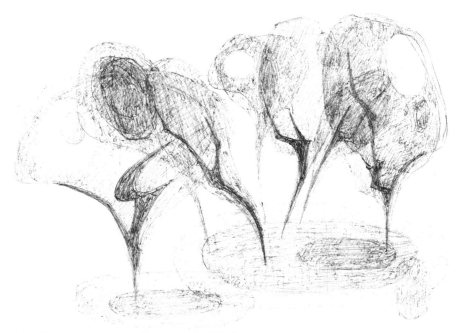

6-2. Working drawing for "Trees in The Wind."

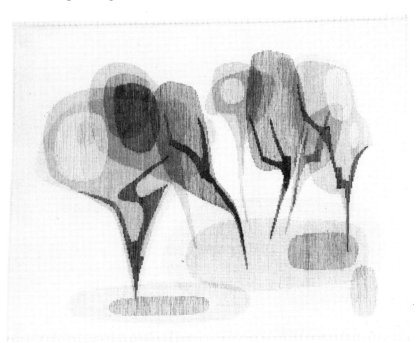

6-3. "Trees in The Wind" — the finished work.

74

Finishing Processes

The moment when the piece of weaving is cut off the loom and first seen in its entirety is a tense one. I try to stand by a rule of *never* doing this at the end of the day when I am tired and probably the light is bad — I can get too depressed!

I find it helpful to have a clear space of light-colored wall in my living room, rather than in my studio, where I can quickly and easily hang the length of fabric and see it in the right plane and probably related to the right background, though this, of course, cannot be assured. I attach much importance to this first moment of my own assessment and appraisal of my work — from it much can be learned. There are the happy times when things appear to have gone well and one experiences a positive and assured reaction. Sometimes, however, one is pervaded by the certainty that all is *not* well, and gloom and depression descend. This is the moment for the neighbors not to drop in! Between the two extremes there are a few occasions of uncertainty. Some color, some value, or some shape seems not quite right, but it is not easy to see exactly where things have gone astray. All, however, may not be lost. I accept as perfectly legitimate the possibility of making alterations to a work where this is absolutely necessary. It can be a slow process but is abundantly rewarding. Using a needle, I insert extra threads alongside the existing inlaid wefts. The result is exactly the same as it would have been had these threads been inlaid in the weave, and a fully satisfactory salvage job can be achieved. Of course, I do not *want* to do this, but it is preferable to scrapping an entire work, and the process of recognizing exactly where the design has gone astray and putting right the fault is not without its own satisfactions. I can think of more than one of my more successful hangings that have been through this process. I must add that any alterations of this nature are only acceptable if extra threads are introduced in such a way as to be indistinguishable from those already woven in. It is work that requires patience and accuracy.

The work, having been assessed and occasionally modified in this way, has next to go through various finishing processes. A good press with a steam iron or iron and a damp cloth makes a big difference to the appearance of a fabric. It has the effect of unifying warp and weft into a complete cloth.

Now we have to consider what we are going to do with the two raw edges. It will be noticed that many of my thin linen wall hangings are woven sideways, with the warp lying horizontally in the finished piece. This means that the selvedges are at the top and bottom. My aim in many of these finely woven hangings is for the edges to be as inconspicuous as possible. I like the effect of them fading out into the wall space that surrounds them and feel that a hemmed edge would defeat this aim. I therefore whip the edges with a needle and a length of the weft thread. For this it is necessary to weave a few shots of ground weft at the beginning and end of the hanging which can be cut away after the edge has been sewn.

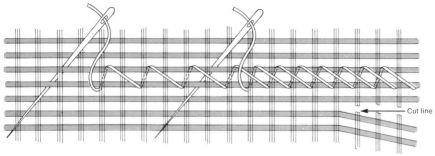

6-4. Method of finishing raw edges.

A neat, reasonably firm, and very inconspicuous edge will now have been created.

Wherever possible I avoid stiffening agents. These tend to stain the fabric, particularly after a lapse of time. In the case of large commissioned work for public buildings, a protective silicone is sometimes sprayed onto the finished work. This makes the fabric a little harsh and unpleasant to handle but does not affect the appearance.

Mounting

Whether a woven hanging is commissioned and therefore destined for a specific setting or is produced speculatively and without one's knowing where it will eventually be hung, it will ultimately have to find its place in a private dwelling or public building and hang from a wall or ceiling. We cannot escape the ultimate link between our work and its architectural environment. We may not always approve of the setting into which our work is ultimately incorporated, but it cannot be eliminated. It is one of the hazards of our profession.

The question of how the work can be hung so as to allow it to fulfil its role as completely as possible should be considered from the start as a part of the total design. At some point some rigid and supporting substance will have to be introduced into the work. What should this be? Metal, wood, glass, and plastic are all possibilities, and all have advantages and disadvantages. Before making a choice from among these substances it is worth considering the unique qualities of a textile as opposed to other objects which hang on our walls. A painting or drawing is essentially rigid with a clearly defined edge or frame, almost always rectangular in shape. This frame tends to isolate it from the wall area. In the case of a textile a single rod or other rigid fitting is usually but not invariably essential, but beyond this we are free to decide on many questions. For example, should the work appear completely rigid or be under a slight degree of tension or entirely slack? Should any necessary attachments be conspicuous or inconspicuous? Will fringes or other continuations of the weave contribute to the total design? Should the work be hung flush with the wall, or right out in the room or a few inches out from the wall so as to create cast shadows, or against a window with the light coming through the work? Although a final decision on these points can be delayed until the work is finished, it is wise to have them under consideration from the start of the project.

My own aim in most of my recent works is that all necessary attachments should be as inconspicuous as possible. This particularly applies to my semitransparent hangings. Bearing in mind my objective that the ultimate rectangle should fade out into the background, it may be helpful to hang it an inch or so out from the wall so that an undefined shadow is cast. In a weave where the design has something of the quality of a sculptor's drawing (for example, Figure 9-6), this indistinct perimeter enhances the solidity and three-dimensional appearance of the central mass.

To achieve these inconspicuous edges I first finish the two raw edges as described above. I then cut two wooden rods to the exact width of the work plus about half an inch. These rods are usually quarter-inch dowel, or as small as they can be to take the weight of the fabric. Fortunately, these thin hangings are extremely light-weight, so the rods need not be large. They need to be painted with a matt-finish paint that matches as closely as possible the fabric to which they will be attached. They are then sewn to the appropriate edges. At this point only, I apply a small quantity of water-diluted P.V.A. adhesive, forming a stiffening agent, to the whipped edges, and particularly to the four corners where the fabric and the rods meet. It should not be allowed to bleed out into the woven fabric.

Methods of hanging are important. Ideally the rod should be supported by two or three small nails, but if it is necessary to hang from the top of the wall, the supporting threads should be as inconspicuous as possible.

I have described here my exact method of finishing the light-weight semitransparent hangings in which I have specialized in recent years. As mentioned above, there are many other ways of finishing fabrics. Some hangings are enhanced by fringes or borders produced by knotting, macramé, or other methods, but these decorations should be a part of the total design and not look like afterthoughts. It is often possible to weave supporting rods into the fabric, and these sometimes form an important feature of the design. Metal rods can look good, but it is important that they should be made of some completely rust-proof material, as metal incorporated with textiles is highly susceptible to rust. Glass or acrylic rods are attractive, though they lack the anonymity of the painted wood, but the fragility of the former is a disadvantage and the latter tend to be very flexible. All decisions on these matters must be individual and relate to the original concept for the work.

chapter 7

COMMISSIONED WORKS, PROBLEMS AND OPPORTUNITIES

I consider myself fortunate in that my work over the last fifteen or more years has been fairly evenly divided between commissioned works, made for a specific purpose and setting, and speculative works, made to exhibit and to sell. The interrelation between the two activities has been stimulating and each has been enriched by the other. While the larger commissioned works have been comparable to the high peaks of a mountain range, the smaller works have been the necessary foothills upon which the whole structure depends. So far in this book I have referred mostly to the foothills. I now wish to describe some of the mountain peaks and the processes, both physical and mental, that led to their creation.

I have heard some artists say that they find the limitations imposed by a commissioned work irritating and frustrating. My own reactions are different. On the whole I find the problems stimulating, though there are, of course, occasions when the conditions are so difficult that it is almost impossible to arrive at a satisfactory solution. The wealth of experience gained from the production of a major work is, of course, immensely valuable. It so happens that the majority of my commissions have been for cathedrals and churches. Most, though not all, the buildings in question have been old, many very old. These buildings, often enlarged and restored at later times, have been subjected over the centuries to wave upon wave of different architectural and design concepts. Individuals and groups of people, knowledgeable or the reverse in aesthetic matters, have, over a long period, been adding to the interiors. Deans and vicars, parochial church councils and mothers' unions, regimental authorities and wealthy donors have all left their mark. It is astonishing how well most of the original buildings have stood up to the invasions of additional furnishings, and certainly the church must always stand as something more than a beautiful artifact but, for a designer asked to produce yet another object, the opposing clutter of centuries adds greatly to the problems.

One aspect of this task which I welcome is the need to establish cordial and sympathetic relations with the people concerned. On first being invited to visit a church in order to discuss a project, I go with a very open mind. My first task is to look and assess and, above all, to meet the people concerned and discuss matters with them. Very often I have been called in on the strength of some casual recommendation and my prospective clients have little or no knowledge of me or my work. It is essential to win their confidence, not only in my photographs and samples of previous work but also in my ability to produce, within the framework of my own artistic integrity, something which will be right for *their* church, not only the building but also the congregation. Once this trust is established I am amazed how responsive people can be to new ideas and abstract designs such as they would probably have rejected previously as impossibly "way out."

After the first visit and discussion I return home to evaluate and think, and this may be the most difficult part of the whole task. Colors and patterns may quarrel; themes, seasons, saints, and symbols must all be given their due consideration. The problem may be a complex one. To arrive at a solution I both draw and weave, producing samples and studies. These drawings and woven samples need to be a good deal more explicit than those described in a previous chapter, which have been prepared only for my own information. They have to be capable of conveying my ideas to my clients with conviction, and I find that a woven study, a complete small work in itself, substantiates the design on paper more convincingly than a mere sample. This study is neither a miniature nor a section of the whole. It is a small woven piece designed in its own right with the same theme, in the same colors, yarns, and textures, forecasting the larger work.

The drawing, probably quite small in scale but prepared with some care, is next shown to the clients, alongside the woven study, and further discussions take place. It is most important to look at the study in the proper setting, as surrounding colors and patterns and lighting arrangements strongly affect the design. Textiles in churches often take the form of altar cloths, and these vary considerably in shape, design, color, and mood. The demands of the architectural settings and the preferences of clients must all be considered.

It often happens that the sanctuary space is cramped and a simple rectangular frontal is the only suitable design. Altars may be fixed to the wall at the back of the sanctuary or may be freestanding — sometimes close to the wall and sometimes out towards the center of the church. There is a present-day move to bring the altar forward in order that the congregation should be more closely involved in the service. This means that the cloth must be designed in the round, and the throwover type is usually preferable. This is, in fact, a large rectangular or near-rectangular table cloth touching the floor all round and with draped corners. If the corners are left as right angles, long points will protrude at the four corners. Sometimes these take up too much floor space and in that case can be rounded off.

The following diagram explains the construction of a throwover and shows how it is woven.

Of the many altar cloths I have designed and woven I have selected three contrasting works to describe in detail. The first is the nave throwover in Manchester Cathedral, the second is in St. James' Church, Oldbury, Worcestershire, and the third is in a newly designed chapel in Ripon Cathedral in Yorkshire.

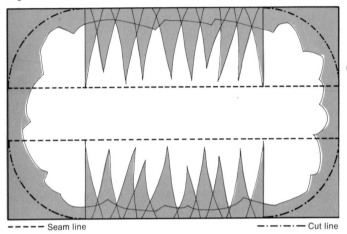

– – – – – Seam line   — · — · — Cut line

7-1.   The construction of an altar throwover.

7-2.   Altar throwover. St. Mary's College, Cheltenham, England.
Photograph by Jones Photography.

The Manchester Altar Throwover

The Manchester Altar throwover is shown in Plate 6 on page 86. The interior of Manchester cathedral is dark and somber. The high walls are composed, inside the building, of red sandstone which has darkened with age and the pollution of an industrial city. In designing an altar cloth for this austere setting, the first problem was to provide a focal point of light and joy. The altar stands almost in the center of the nave and commands attention from all sides. Looking back to this problem I believe my first decision concerned the color, which seemed to me all-important. The building has a fine modern stained-glass window which is almost entirely flame and orange in color, and I was so struck by the vibrancy of this glass in relation to the color of the walls that I decided to echo it in the altar cloth. Massive areas of silver were added to the orange ground color. The color and texture variations in these silver areas were produced by inlaying handmade yarns of the type described in Chapter 5. Most contain a certain amount of metallic thread, and accents of light result from the addition of small strips of silver plastic to the inlaid areas. Normally I avoid the use of metallics, as these can all too easily appear meretritious, but the dark interiors of churches call for some over-dramatization. The flame color of the ground continues on the reverse side of the altar and terminates in an uneven border. A dark handwoven braid edges the entire cloth, and the corners are cut to quarter circles. The natural stretch of the fabric on the diagonal produces the fan shape of the draped corners. It is woven in the Moorman technique and fibers used include wool, cotton, filament rayon, and metallics.

The design of the throwover derives from a series of drawings of rock formations on a wild stretch of coast in Wales, and the theme is one of strength and endurance.

The Oldbury Throwover

The Oldbury throwover is illustrated in Plate 8 on page 87. Structurally this cloth is made on the same lines as that at Manchester, but in other respects it differs widely. The Oldbury church is modern and situated in a new housing development in the heart of the industrial Midlands. Here there was no problem of light to contend with, as the church has large clear glass windows and the daylight is strong. The altar is large and occupies a prominent forward position in the sanctuary. The building is spacious and uncluttered. I was first asked to suggest a design for a Festal cloth, that is, the cloth used at the great church festivals, for which the traditional colors are white and yellow, silver and gold. On finding that the church also lacked a Trinity frontal, that is, the green frontal mostly in use at other times of the year, it was suggested that the two themes might possibly be incorporated in one cloth. Finally a design was submitted with a Festal theme on one half and a Trinity theme on the other. The cloth thus can be

1. Door hanging. The Priest's House, Elkstone, Gloucestershire, England.

2. Necklace. Silk, metallic thread, and natural stones with mica.

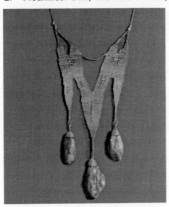

3. "Herb Robert and Rock," wall hanging. 15 in. x 30 in. Linen and wool.

turned round (*not* over) to suit the different church seasons. Though both fronts are at all times visible, only one is seen at the appropriate season by the congregation.

I was aware of the need to weld the two fronts, with their different themes and colors, into one total unit. The design for the Festal half, shown in the photograph, has a dynamic quality based on flame shapes, whereas the other side is more static, suggestive of slow and natural growth. The problem of color was difficult to solve, particularly the choice of a common background color that would link the yellows on one side and the greens on the other and would also look right with the fairly distinct blue of the santuary wall. In the end a soft and pale blue-gray seemed the right solution. The four draped corners are all yellow and the points of the rectangles are allowed to protrude, forming an interesting pattern as they unite with the design of the sanctuary steps. The Moorman technique was again used, and the yarns are varied, though no metallic threads were introduced.

Ripon Cathedral Altar Frontal

At the time when the Ripon Cathedral cloth was commissioned, plans for constructing a new chapel within the old framework of the cathedral were well advanced. A craftsman in metal had already designed and made an elaborate screen at the entrance to the chapel and also a pair of altar rails (see Plate 4, page 86). The design of these is dynamic and, coupled with the brilliance of the new metal alloy employed, is perhaps disturbing in the majestic setting. The altar cloth was envisaged as the only area of strong color in the chapel, and it seemed to need a design that had a restful and even a static quality in contrast to the dynamic design of the metalwork. It was, however, important that there should be some link between the static and dynamic design concepts. The design adopted is dominated by shapes that are enclosed and roughly curved, drawing the eye to the center of the altar, but it also includes a secondary theme which echoes, in a series of shadowy shapes, the lightning-flash theme of the metal. In the final work a dark shadow appears to be cast by the altar rails upon the brilliant reds, oranges, and yellows of the frontal. The cloth is a simple rectangle, inlaid in Moorman technique with threads that are predominantly wool. I had often produced the effect of a shadow *behind* some dominant form in my design, but the need to suggest a shadow *on top* of the form necessitated a modification in cloth structure and threading that I have used subsequently to obtain a similar effect. It is in ways such as this that a solution to a problem imposed by a commissioned work can add to our creative abilities.

In addition to altar cloths I have carried out many commissions for textiles designed for other purposes, for both ecclesiastical and other buildings. Some of them are described below.

A Three-Dimensional Hanging

The large hall in this church school includes a sanctuary which is set back within the main rectangle and can be shut off by folding doors when not in use. Above these doors is a large area of wall and it is here that my work hangs, forming a link between the hall and the sanctuary. I was specifically asked to base my design on the theme of the crucifixion but to include the forecast of hope and joy as well as tragedy. How was this to be attempted in a piece of weaving? Here was a need for an abstract design which was still capable of conveying a theme or mood.

I was at this time experimenting outside my normal technique with three-dimensional works composed of single or groups of hanging forms, woven in tapestry technique to the required shapes, and the proposed commission enabled me to use my ideas in the production of a major work (see Plate 5, page 86). The total hanging is eight feet high by nine and a half feet wide and consists of three separate suspended units woven to these dimensions and hanging one in front of another with an eight-inch space between each. The whole work hangs clear of the back wall by a space of eight inches. Each piece is attached to aluminum rods at top and bottom, but there is no rigid edge at the sides, so each section hangs freely. A series of key warp threads in extremely strong linen twine occur at six-inch intervals and provide the structure which holds everything in position. These threads can be seen as faint vertical lines in the reproduction.

The center layer is the main one. The orange-red cross dominates the work and is flanked by two subsidiary crosses. The supporting groups of woven forms convey the idea of watching and waiting figures in the simplest possible way. The back layer is composed of fairly large areas of weaving. These are dark and shadowy and echo the theme of the cross. The front layer needed to be very open so that the center would not be obscured. It consists of spear shapes, the dark ones rising from the base and appearing to fight the silver ones descending from the top. It could suggest a battle between good and evil through which the main drama is seen.

The need to evoke a theme or a mood through both the opportunities and the limitations of the technique was, in this work, realized to the full, and this exemplifies a point I have dwelt on previously. I refer to the perfect synthesis between the conception and the technique which should, I consider, be our goal.

Details of the technique employed in the production of this work are given in Chapter 8.

4. Altar frontal. Chapel of the Holy Spirit, Ripon Cathedral, England.

5. "The Crucifixion," three-dimensional hanging. Agnes Stewart School, Leeds, England.   9 ft. 6 in. x 8 ft. x 16 in.

6. Altar throwover. Manchester Cathedral, England.

7. "Two Stones," wall hanging. 30 in. x 38 in. Linen and cotton.

8. Altar throwover. St. James' Church, Oldbury, Worcestershire, England.

Two Space Dividers

This commission posed problems of quite a different sort. It was desired to convert a large top-story room into three sections which could be used as young people's bedrooms. The fine old house, once connected with a monastery, has magnificent roof beams and from the outset these dominated the design. The woven areas would be large, and available money was very limited, so I was aware from the start that it would be a "budget job." The technique therefore needed to be one that would be comparatively quick to carry out. I turned here to the cloth structure explained in Chapter 3. There was still a fine tie-down warp in use but the weft was two-ply rug wool, and weaving the plain or nearly plain areas proceeded at a good speed. The design was dictated by the dominant shapes of the beams. In order to weave the hangings to the right shapes, very accurate measurements had to be taken and methods of suspension had to be carefully devised.

7-3. Two space dividers. Ashleworth Court, Gloucestershire, England. Photograph by Jones Photography.

At the end of Chapter 5 I referred to the unexpected gifts, the bonuses, that sometimes come one's way. One of these emerged from this work. The total room space is a rectangle, about thirty-six feet by fifteen feet, and the two hangings split this up into three sections, each about twelve feet by fifteen feet. The only windows are in the two short walls at each end of the total area, and thus the center section is rather dark in contrast with the other two sections. A characteristic of my technique is that the inlaid pattern appears on one side of the fabric only, and naturally the decorated surfaces were made to face the two windows. I was expecting the "walls" of the center area to be undecorated, but when all was in place I found, to my surprise and pleasure, that the inlay showed plainly through the nonopaque cloth as a monochrome design. This shows very clearly in the photograph.

Door Curtain
This hanging (see Plate 1, page 82) fills an aperture between a room and a passage. It is woven mainly in wool in Moorman technique. A light metal frame supports the fabric in the top area and this is hinged to the stone doorway so that the hanging, although not rigid, forms a door which can be opened and closed. The house is a very old structure and the rugged stones forming the archway are arresting and impressive in shape. The design of the hanging is based on rock forms and the link between the woven piece and the surrounding stonework is obvious.

The five works described above in some detail have all added enrichment to my experience and creative abilities in one or more ways. The design for the Manchester throwover required the rough silver textural areas and led to the idea of the specially prepared wefts for inlay described in Chapter 5. The two-sided Oldbury throwover produced unique color problems. The Ripon frontal led to a variation in the cloth structure to produce the effect of a superimposed shadow.

All the other projects mentioned here, and many more, have added to my store of knowledge. Nearly all have taxed my ingenuity on the subject of assembling, fitting, and mounting, and these negative points, which are only right when are unnoticeable, are of much importance. Working out what could almost be described as the engineering problems in the Leeds three-dimensional hanging caused me more than one sleepless night.

One problem common to all these works is the need for durability. I was interested and a little apprehensive when I visited the school in Leeds five years after the three-dimensional hanging was installed. It had been untouched since it was made. I was relieved to find it in good shape.

There was no sign of threads sagging or of the three panels being out of alignment. A good deal of dust had gathered, as was to be expected. (When the work was completed, it was treated with a silicone protective agent, and I hope that when it is possible to clean the whole work, it will be found that the dust is on the surface only and has not penetrated the fabric.) On other occasions I have been less happy on seeing my work after a lapse of time.

Modern thought tends to immediacy. "Have now, pay later" is our creed, and in gaining the appearance we desire, it is all too easy to brush aside considerations of what our work will look like in five or ten years' time. I do not suggest that durability should be an overriding aim. It can be argued that textiles have in any case a limited life span, and that if they give pleasure for a number of years they will have fulfilled their function. My concern is not so much with their elimination as with their shabbiness. If a work is given decent burial after an honorable life, well and good, but if, as only too often happens, it remains in poor condition, gathering dust like last winter's dried flower arrangement and losing the subtle tensions of the original design, then I feel distressed. This is especially apt to happen in the case of works with a fragile and ephemeral character. The great tapestries of the past, the outcome of a long tradition of craftsmanship, have maintained their nobility over the centuries. Will our modern hangings fare so well?

chapter 8

SOME OTHER TECHNIQUES FOR WOVEN HANGINGS

Most of this book has been devoted to uses and variations of a specific inlay technique, and I have, over a long period, found this an absorbing and fertile field for experiment and study. It is not, however, the only technique I use, and in this final chapter I refer to various others that have absorbed my attention from time to time.

An outstanding example of my employment of a different technique for a specific purpose is the three-dimensional hanging in the Agnes Stewart School in Leeds, referred to in the previous chapter. Although the concept for this work emanated from previous design and technical experiments, the scale and positioning immediately posed new problems. The total weight of the work is considerable, and toughness and strength in the fabric as well as in the supports were required. A traditional tapestry structure woven with thick, closely packed wefts on a very strong linen warp was selected, and this provided great intensity of color as well as strength and durability. The woven areas are about the thickness and strength of a heavy tapestry rug. The design needed a considerable break-up of color and texture in the larger areas and also some focal points. The latter were introduced in the form of blocks of Ghiordes knots, producing a heavy pile, and were designed to stand out as light areas from the rich reds and blues of the principal section of the work.

As the loom on which I was weaving was only thirty inches wide, the design had to be planned in sections which were later joined together. A normal tapestry warp, composed of a strong linen thread, was set up but only woven across in the shapes required, the remainder of the warp being left unwoven. These warp threads were subsequently knotted together in pairs and darned back into the fabric. Only a series of extra-strong warps at six-inch intervals remained, and they formed the key structure on which everything depends.

The proper mounting of the work posed a problem, and in the end the following method was adopted. At the top and bottom of each of the three layers is an aluminum strip with a box-shaped cross section and into the box fits an aluminum rod. The "key" warp threads pass through holes drilled at six-inch intervals in the box strip and are tied to the rod with adjustable knots. This made a neat finish with no ragged ends of threads visible, and also made tension adjustment possible when the work was assembled.

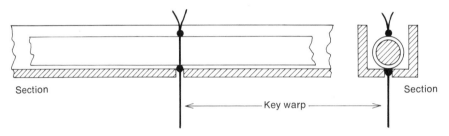

Section   Section

← ——————————— Key warp ——————————— →

8-1. Method of mounting three-dimensional hanging. Agnes Stewart School, Leeds.

The method of designing this hanging presented another problem. It was not only necessary for me to be able to read my own design but also for my clients to get a correct idea of what I had in mind. I worked out the design on three sheets of glass measuring fourteen inches by twelve inches and worked with special paints and crayons that would adhere to the glass surface. The sheets were then set up on blocks of wood, one behind the other, at the correct distances apart and thus formed an explicit model of the final work. In addition to the model, I prepared several preliminary woven studies.

I intended to draw again on larger sheets of paper from the glass model, analyzing the design and preparing a more exact cartoon to work from, but in the end I was frightened of losing something of the first spark and impetus that had gone into the painting on glass, so I decided, I think rightly, to weave direct from the small glass panels.

The technique employed in the weaving lends itself also to the production of smaller works, and other developments can arise from it. I became interested in the possibility of *using* the unwoven warp threads to continue the design, forming patterns and tensions outside the positive woven areas.

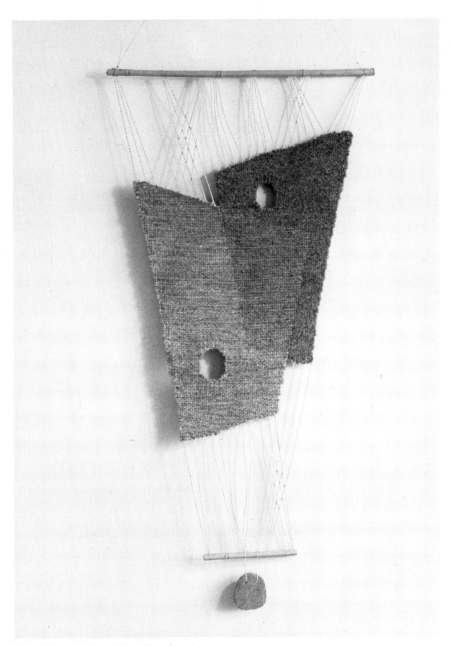

8-2. "Lime & Grey," free-form hanging.

A growing interest in weaving nonrectangular shapes forces upon us the need for both technical complexities and simplicities. Adaptations of and additions to the loom may be required, but at the same time we begin to be aware of the freedom inherent in the simplest of all cloth structures, namely, the plain weave of traditional tapestry. A loom can be a simple frame or an elaborate multiharness structure. The elaborations add to and subtract from the design possibilities. For example, a beater and reed are needed for weaving a length of cloth, but if we discard these things we are immediately free from the restrictions of the rectangle.

Finger manipulation of wefts may be slow but also provides the weaver with immense freedom. Subtle variations of color and texture can be introduced on the spur of the moment. Threads need not necessarily run parallel or at right angles to the warp, and other possibilities of weaving free forms emerge.

I have been interested in the developments that can arise from a fan-shaped arrangement of warp threads. Starting from a group of, say, twenty-four threads attached to the cloth beam at the front of the loom, the threads can be entered in two or more harnesses and fanned out evenly before being attached to the warp beam. On this fan-shaped warp various pointed forms can be woven. These can vary in size from large sculptural hangings to dress pendants and necklaces such as the one shown on Plate 2, page 83. I have produced both.

Weaving in this way demands a progressive change in the size of the weft. When the warp threads are bunched tightly together a very fine weft is used, but as the warp threads become farther apart the warp size must be increased in order to provide adequate filling. I keep adding more and more fine threads to the original one until I am weaving with a bunch of perhaps twenty fine threads all stranded together to form one quite substantial weft. This method lends itself to great subtleties of color blending.

These pendant-hangings call for some form of weight and, in fact, the choice of a suitable object for this purpose can be a starting point for a design. There are many attractive possibilities such as natural stones, both polished and unpolished, specially designed pottery weights, objects of metal, glass, or wood. I find great pleasure in collecting pebbles and stones with special beauties of color, pattern, form, and texture and incorporating them in my work, drawing out from them subtle color schemes so that the stone and the weaving appear fully integrated. The method of joining the stone to the weaving poses quite a problem. With a soft stone it is possible to drill a hole in it, but if the stone is hard I find it is best to weave a tiny cap, like an inverted basket, and attach this to the stone with epoxy resin.

Larger pendant-hangings produced in this way can be grouped in interesting ways to form three-dimensional works.

Other experiments with a fan-shaped warp carried out some years ago involved the use of a specially prepared reed. This was itself formed like a fan (Figure 8-3). It was not fixed in the beater but was suspended from the top of the loom on cords which could be easily adjusted in length. Weaving was started with the reed in a high position so the warp threads were forced closely together, forming a narrow web. The reed was then lowered by gradual stages so that the warp was constantly widening. In the piece shown in Figure 8-4 four harnesses were used, so that it was possible to weave a double cloth forming pockets into which flat pebbles could be inserted.

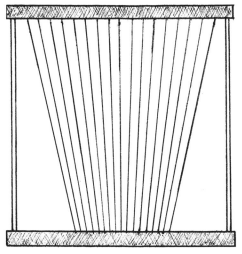

8-3. Fan-shaped reed.

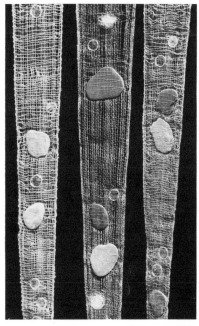

8-4. Transparent hanging with inset pebbles.

The experiments referred to in this chapter and indeed in this whole book represent only a tiny section of the great expanse of opportunities open to textile artists today. I referred in an earlier chapter to the star formation at the center of which we are placed. As our experiments grow, we become more and more aware of the radial paths all around us.

We are faced with many questions. Shall we fulfill our function as weavers to the greatest advantage by selecting one path only and pursuing it in depth, or shall we do better to explore all around us in many directions but inevitably in a less specialized way? Having chosen the way of specialization, I am strongly aware that we never come to the end of the track. As our experience grows and we obtain freedom from technical difficulties, the problems and opportunities intensify and our decisions, especially concerning the crucial problem of the right design for the technique, become more critical. A knife edge can divide a correct from an incorrect judgment.

In some weavers the desire to learn and use a large number of new techniques is very strong, and therefore they explore outwards in many directions rather than pursue the one long road of specialization. Neither one nor the other of these ways of working is right or wrong. Everything depends on the personalities and aspirations of individual men and women. We are all free to decide.

chapter 9

GALLERY OF WORKS
BY THE AUTHOR

9-1. "Black & Blue Abstract," wall hanging.
32 in. x 38 in. Linen and cotton.

9-2. "Dark Form," wall hanging.
30 in. x 65 in. Linen and cotton.

9-3. "Trees," wall hanging. 25 in. x 38 in. Linen and cotton.

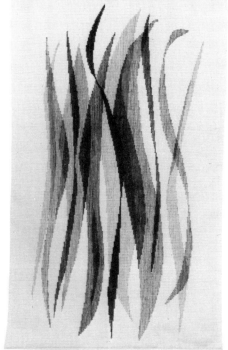

9-4. "Grasses," wall hanging. 32 in. x 38 in. Linen and cotton.

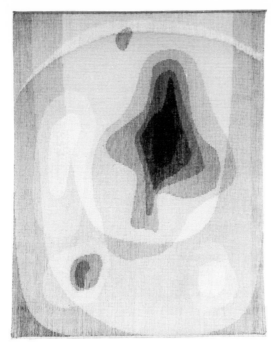

9-5. "Underwater Pattern," wall hanging. 36 in. x 38 in.
Linen and cotton.

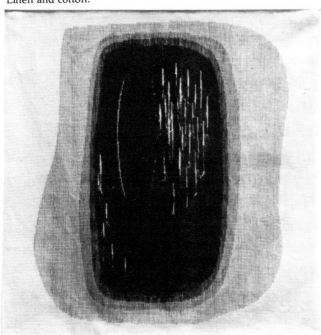

9-6. "Black Oval," wall hanging. 38 in. x 38 in. Linen and cotton.

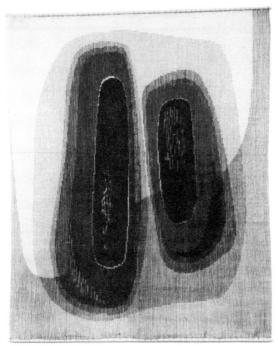

9-7. "Two Ovals," wall hanging. 30 in. x 38 in.
Linen, cotton, and wool.

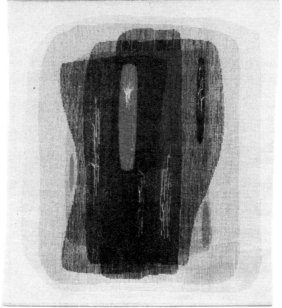

9-8. "Orange Abstract," wall hanging. 33 in. x 38 in.
Linen, cotton, and wool.

9-9. "Pierced Landscape," wall hanging. 25 in. x 38 in.
Linen, cotton, and wool.

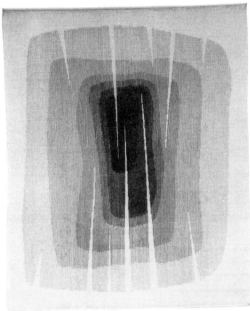

9-10. "Pierced Form," wall hanging. 30 in. x 38 in.
Linen and cotton.

Portrait of the Author. Photograph by Nicholas Large.

INDEX

103